DEDIC

To Chauncey C. Riddle, with respect, gratitude, and affection.

MISSION STATEMENT

The function of this guide is to enhance reaching the goal of quality estate planning with trusts, which is to maximize the individual and family control of their wealth, minimize the costs and complexities in the care of each individual and the estate, and minimize the imposition of all forms of transfer taxes.

QUICK PREP

Generating an Effective Estate Plan with a Living Trust

What You Need to Know

George M. Turner

ISBN 978-0-314-28683-3

Mat #41386977

CONTENTS

Preface

The eminent Harvard law professor, A. James Casner, once stated:

"The impact of a new tax law upon estate planning is most directly related to the savings of taxes. Yet it is clear that the savings of taxes is only one consideration among many in estate planning and, consequently, that the plan which results in the least tax burden is not always the best plan."[1]

The intent of this guide is to examine those pertinent issues regarding estate planning through trusts, which will not simply address the subject of taxation. The subject matter of the dignity of the individual and family will be emphasized. Techniques will be explored whereby individuals and families are allowed to maximize control of their estates, minimize the cost of administration and taxation, and maintain the dignity of all individuals through proper documents available for public use without the need of the courts.

It is hoped that through the exploration of the techniques available in estate planning that the dignity of the individual will be maximized, the cost of estate management taxation will be minimized, the control of the family affairs will be enhanced, and the intrusion into the privacy of the individual and family will be minimized.

---

[1] A. James Casner,, *Estate Planning Under the Revenue Act of 1948*, 62 HARV. L. REV. 413 (1949).

1

Overview of the Estate Planning Process

Staying in Control and Uses of Professionals

The purpose of this book is to help you establish a quality estate planning through an attorney or financial advisor by tailoring a plan to your particular needs. However, you should always maintain control of both your financial affairs and your person.

The role of attorneys and financial advisors is to function as your servants. You should always make the final decisions. Their responsibility is to provide you with appropriate and necessary options from which you can make a determination as to what your best interests are and what meets the correct criteria for your family's needs.

The Two Subjects of Estate Planning

Reduced to its simplest components, estate planning addresses only two basic categories for any individual or family, namely:

1. Your person
2. Your wealth

It is commonly said that death and taxes are the only immutable characteristics of this life. Given the present status of our tax law, it has become apparent that the vast majority of families in the United States can avoid death taxes with proper planning. Hence, only death still remains inevitable.

The emphasis of this guide is not to address the 1 percent of individuals or families with unique financial problems. Rather, the emphasis will be on the 99 percent for whom estate planning issues are more commonplace. Too often, those responsible for estate planning appear preoccupied with esoteric situations that rarely apply to the general public. Far too little has been written suggesting estate planning methods applicable to the vastly larger segment of the population, which, by its sheer numbers, is in greater need of competent planning.

Defining the Two Categories

The general categories of "your person" and "your wealth" can be reduced to even more basic usable documents.

Issue #1 - Your Person

1. Power of attorney for health care
2. Living will declaration or directive to physicians or do not resuscitate
3. Burial or cremation directive
4. Donation of body parts

Issue #2 - Your Wealth

1. Nothing: i.e., intestacy
2. Joint tenancy or tenants by the entirety
3. Wills

   a. attested formal form
   b. holographic – handwritten

4. Beneficiary designation (e.g., life insurance, Totten trust or IRA or pension plan)
5. Trusts

Turner's Three Laws

Since estate planning is conceptually this simple, then you only need to address what is, for want of a better term, "Turner's Three Laws."

Turner's First Law

In probate, expenses expand to consume the money available.

Turner's Second Law

The level of avarice of children rises to its highest level on the death of a parent. Turner's Second Law has a corollary to it, which is, that the acrimony among siblings increases geometrically to the length of time to close and distribute an estate.

Turner's Third Law

Maximization for employment of attorneys and accountants in estate planning increases proportionately to the number of days Congress is in session each year.

Although the three laws intend some humor, the problems described are very real. Recognition of these realities will assist to analyze and develop the best techniques to help your family maximize savings and harmony.

What Are Your Desires?

Most writers emphasize that the principal motivations for estate planning are the following seven items:

1. Minimizing the cost of estate settlement
2. Minimizing the time of estate settlement
3. Minimizing the complexity of estate settlement
4. Minimizing the total tax liability of the estate
5. Maximizing the family's privacy

6. Providing adequate management and control, both during the
   lifetime and after the death of either or both spouses
7. Minimizing the likelihood of contests during estate settlement

As this writer has matured in the practice of law, it has become apparent
that the preceding list does not accurately represent the true essence of
why people seek quality estate planning. The following list of estate
planning aims and priorities is far more accurate, both in terms of
analysis and priorities.

1. Maximize control
2. Maximize access
3. Maximize preservation during the lives of both spouses
4. Maximize quality management
5. Maximize family privacy
6. Minimize time of estate settlement
7. Minimize complexity of estate settlement
8. Minimize cost of estate settlement
9. Minimize taxes of estate settlement
10. Minimize time of distribution of estate to desired beneficiaries

In presenting these two different lists to people without revealing the
source, time and again and without exception, each person has adamantly
claimed the second list of ten items to be far more important to them.

Finally, as even the title of this book suggests, the emphasis is on the use
of living trusts as a vehicle to guide you in achieving both necessary and
quality estate planning for you and your family.

Failure to utilize the basic principles outlined in this book could result in:

1. The loss of substantial amounts of family wealth;
2. Grief and heartache due to a complicated and outdated probate
   settlement system;
3. Dissipation of family wealth stemming from the use of
   conservatorship in the event of your inability to take care of
   yourself if disabled; and

4. Your children possibly receiving far less from family by inadequate planning.

Thankfully, the capacity to accomplish quality estate planning is within your reach. It is simply a matter of engaging the proper counsel to implement the requisite documentation that has been both well developed and made available to those practitioners who are bona fide professional estate planners.

2

Options Available in the Estate Planning Process

Introduction

A broad definition of estate planning encompasses not only personal desires and quality tax planning, but also proper drafting of documents and thorough implementation of all aspects of the arrangements made. This will ensure that the family's wealth is passed to desired beneficiaries with minimum settlement cost and taxation.

The first goal, which can be accomplished by using revocable trusts, is to provide the husband and wife—as a couple or as single individuals—with two guarantees. The first is the ability to maintain total control over their property throughout their lives. The second is a carefully planned distribution after they have died.

The second goal in the broad overview of estate planning, which can be accomplished by using irrevocable trusts, is to provide the best possible technique for making gifts to individuals in trust. An irrevocable trust can be used to ensure proper control, to shift income taxation, and to maximize the effectiveness of making gifts to charitable institutions.

Beginning with the 1981 Reagan Tax Act, also known as ERTA, effective January 1, 1982, and the adoption of the Tax Relief Act of 1997, and the Tax Relief, Unemployment Insurance Reauthorization, and Job Creation Act, which passed December 16, 2010, combined with the inherent characteristics of trusts, has made it possible to guarantee that a family (with proper documentation) can realize the following ten benefits:

1. Continued control over their assets during their lifetime, just as if no particular estate-planning document were in force
2. Continued access to family wealth
3. Maximization of family privacy during life and after the passing of an individual or both spouses
4. Elimination of the need to use courts for the appointment of a conservator or guardian
5. A present minimum exemption of $5 million per person grows. This is only through 2013. After that, even that the gods do not know
6. Deferral of all taxation until both spouses have died
7. Passage of the property to desired beneficiaries
8. Avoidance of the cost of probate
9. Avoidance of the time and frustration involved in probate
10. Maximization of tax savings, at least in the short term

These desirable ends are relatively simple in concept, but to understand the techniques by which they can best be accomplished, it is important to first understand how most property is transferred at death.

Transferring Property at Death

The five most commonly used means of transferring property at death are as follows:

1. *Intestacy*—This simply means that an individual has no formal planning; about 65 percent of people in the United States die intestate.
2. *Joint Tenancy*—This means transfer of property held by two or more persons from the decedent (the person who died) to the survivor. Another version of this for couples in some states is *tenancy by the entirety.*
3. *Beneficiary Designation* or *Totten Trust*—This is a transfer of property by the naming of a beneficiary under a life insurance policy, pension plan, an annuity, or under a trustee bank account commonly known as a Totten Trust.

4. *Will*—This is a document drafted by an attorney or an individual that designates the transfer of property to those named. It is an arrangement that must be probated in the courts. (The general use of handwritten or a holographic will is not encouraged.)

5. *Trust*—These are of two varieties: (a) *living trust* (or *inter vivos* trust), which is brought into existence during lifetime, or (b) *testamentary trust,* which is included within the terms of a will and is brought into existence when probate is completed.

Because some estimates suggest that about 98 percent of property transfers at death are handled through these methods, only these methods will be examined in this book.

Attempts have been made to reduce all definitions to simple language, and a glossary is provided for reference. Although some definitions may be criticized as oversimplified, there is enough information here to give you a clear understanding of estate planning for your personal use. The professionals of your choice can provide details and specifics.

An Overview of the Five Basic Approaches

Again, the five basic estate planning approaches for passing property at death include intestacy, joint tenancy (or tenancy by the entirety), naming of beneficiaries, wills, and trusts.

Intestate Succession (Doing Nothing)

Passage of property by intestate succession takes place when an individual or family fails to write either a will or a trust instrument directing how the property is to be distributed.

Under the intestacy arrangements of every state in the United States, local law generally provides that most or all of the estate will be transferred to the surviving spouse. In some states, the estate will be divided between the spouse and the living children. If there is not a surviving spouse, the property is usually distributed equally among the children. If both the spouse and the children have passed away, the property usually passes to the grandchildren.

Intestacy laws vary from state to state, but, as a general rule, property will eventually be distributed to some family member—even if it is a distant cousin.

The possibility that an estate will revert to the state of *domicile* (state of permanent residence) of the person who has died is extremely remote. Property reverting to the state is referred to as an *escheatment*. It is an unlikely possibility that is sadly overplayed by those attempting to scare people into buying suspect Form Book Documents or preprinted documents.

Disadvantages of Intestacy

There are two primary disadvantages to using a state's intestacy laws. First, it will mean at least one probate, and usually two probates. One probate will be required at the death of the first spouse and another at the death of the surviving spouse. The expense and time factors, along with family disputes that are inherent in the probate system, will be discussed at length in Chapter 3.

The second disadvantage depends on the size of the estate. If the estate is of substantial size, intestacy may cause what is known as *double taxation*. The impact of double taxation on an estate will be discussed in Chapter 4. The passage of property to desired beneficiaries through intestacy is probably, in most cases, the worst approach to estate planning, although it is the most common. Some estimates suggest that 65 percent of estates have no planning; hence, the laws of intestate determine who will be beneficiaries.

Joint Tenancy (or Tenancy by the Entirety)

Joint tenancy is one of those classic English common law fictions that cannot be, but it works. Illustration 2-1 should be helpful in explaining the concept.

Illustration 2-1 During the Life of Husband and Wife

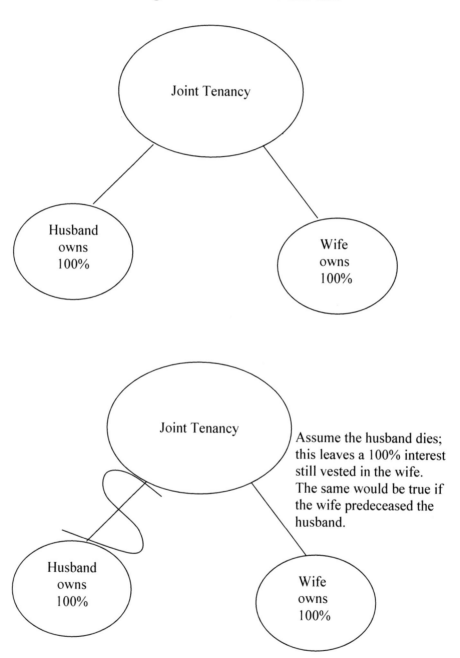

Joint Tenancy

Husband owns 100%

Wife owns 100%

Joint Tenancy

Assume the husband dies; this leaves a 100% interest still vested in the wife. The same would be true if the wife predeceased the husband.

Husband owns 100%

Wife owns 100%

For example, if a husband and wife own their home in joint tenancy, the fiction is that each spouse simultaneously owns 100 percent of the property. Obviously, this is impossible because it would mean that two individuals can each own 100 percent of the property at the same time or that there is actually 200 percent of the property. Clearly, both possibilities are fictional.

However, joint tenancy is a very useful fiction. If one spouse dies, it is usually not necessary to probate the assets because there is a surviving spouse who owns 100 percent of the property. Hence, there is no need for determination of ownership.

Some attorneys still probate joint tenancy. This is sometimes done under the guise of proving that one spouse has died. This actually happened at my father's death. Occasionally, some form of probate may be necessary to establish the correct status or character of ownership. This is particularly true in the community property states, where joint tenancy and community property are treated as inconsistent methods of holding property. In the community property states, probate of joint tenancy property may be important and totally justified, but not always. If in doubt, obtain a second opinion.

If all property is held in joint tenancy, the same disadvantages arise as when property is transferred by intestacy. This situation will create at least one probate on the death of the second spouse, and it will automatically force the family into the unfortunate situation of double taxation if the estate is large enough to be affected by estate tax.

Given those assets now included in estates for federal estate tax purposes, and in many cases for state inheritance tax purposes, it takes only an estate of average size to create a double taxation effect. So, even if you are not a multimillionaire, this can have a significant effect on you. As will be demonstrated in Chapter 4, the double taxation effect may still be a serious issue for the average citizen.

Tenancy by the entirety has the same characteristics as joint tenancy except that it is used exclusively between a husband and wife, whereas any two or more persons can use joint tenancy.

Beneficiary Designation, Totten Trusts, and Annuities

A life insurance product has the advantage of totally avoiding probate when there is a named beneficiary. If the proceeds are left directly to the surviving spouse, however, this usually creates double taxation on the surviving spouse's death.

Probate can be avoided by establishing an account at a banking institution that has a named beneficiary. This arrangement is known as a Totten trust.

Just as a beneficiary can be named on a life insurance product or on a Totten trust, a beneficiary can be named on some forms of pension plans, or annuities, where there is a residual benefit to be passed on to another individual upon the death of the annuitant. These vary from common corporate pension plans to privately owned annuities and individual retirement accounts (IRA).

Wills

One type of will is a *formal will*, which is a written document normally prepared by an attorney. Unfortunately, wills may also be purchased in a stationery store, often in a form using a boilerplate drafting technique. The substantive provisions within the printed forms are often inadequately or incompetently drafted for a particular jurisdiction. Frequently, they do not provide guidelines on how they must be signed and witnessed. Those facts alone make the use of such documents highly suspect, if not foolish.

With the increase of computers and the proliferation of software, it should be no surprise that there are a number of computer will-writing programs available. Those that offer simplified, do-it-yourself will-writing techniques may have all the disadvantages of the preprinted forms. It is unfortunate that the sophistication of software can produce a professional look that is not always supported by the content. When information supplied by the user is incorporated into the document and printed, there may be no evidence that a fill-in-the-blank format was used. This can end up being a very subtle form of deception, intended or not, by the designer of the software.

It is in your best interest to spend the comparatively small amount of money to obtain the services of a competent estate planning attorney, even in the preparation of a simple will. The savings to your estate is worth the cost.

The two elements of a formal will are:

1. It is properly drafted in accordance with the laws in the state in which the testator resides; and
2. Two or three people witness the signing of the will, according to formalities dictated by state law, and add their signatures as witnesses.

Most wills between spouses are of a reciprocal nature. That is, when one spouse dies, he or she leaves the entire estate to the surviving spouse. In the event of the death of both, the property is often distributed to the children.

If this approach is used, the family is faced with the same kind of problems that exist in the intestacy situation. There will be a potential probate on the death of both the husband and the wife, as well as the probability of double taxation.

Another common type of will is the *handwritten (holographic) will*. By definition, a handwritten will (or holographic will) normally contains three elements:

1. It is written wholly in the handwriting of the testator;
2. It is dated by the testator; and
3. It is signed by the testator.

These requirements obviously preclude the use of witnesses or notarization. Although it is commonly believed that all wills must bear the signature of witnesses, use of a witness or notarization on this type of will usually ensures that the document will not be treated or considered as a will by the courts. It becomes simply a piece of paper with writing on it without legal effect.

A classic example of this problem occurred when a gentleman, who was traveling through his home state, stopped at a motel for the night. Having a premonition that he would not live through the night, he sat down to write his will on a piece of motel stationery.

The document was indeed wholly in his handwriting, signed and dated by him. Unfortunately, in the upper right hand corner, shown in Illustration 2-2, was printed the motel's name and address. The Supreme Court of the state declared this was not a will because there was printing on the page. Hence, the document was not wholly in the gentleman's handwriting. The document was held to be simply a piece of paper with writing on it, with no legal effect on the distribution of his property.

Illustration 2-2

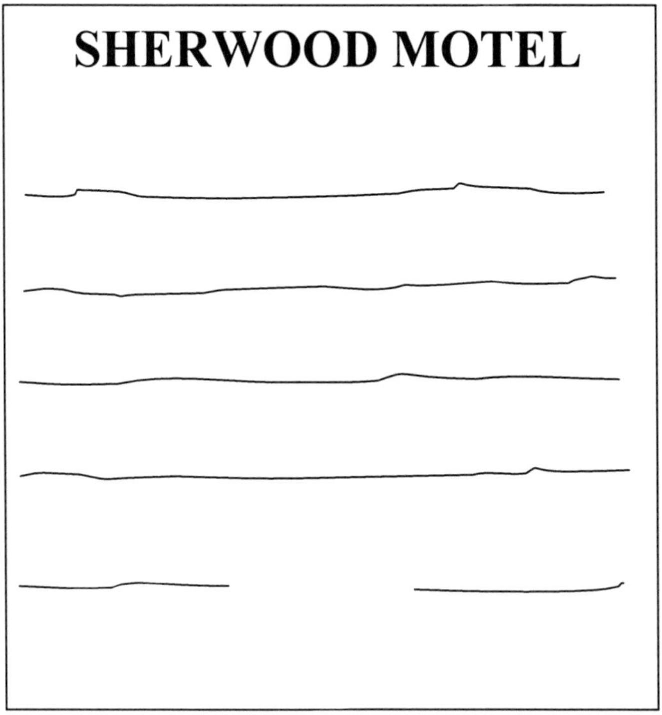

Perhaps the most tragic example of an attempted holographic will was a situation where a woman wrote a six-page, handwritten document in careful form, using all the correct legal words. It appeared that she was legally trained or at least a very competent student. Unfortunately, to ensure that it was indeed her handwriting, she requested that a neighbor sign as a witness.

With only one witness and not two, as required by that particular state, the document was not considered a formal will. The State Supreme Court also held that the document was not wholly in her handwriting and therefore, not a holographic will either.

The intent of this well-drafted document was to distribute her estate to three relatives. Instead, her estate went to seventeen persons under the laws of intestacy. It came out during the trial that she did not even know twelve of the seventeen beneficiaries.

Use of a Revocable Trust

The only known method that will guarantee transfer of all assets of an estate without necessity of probate and that will protect the estate from double taxation is the use of a revocable living trust. The details of the establishment and workings of that trust system will be covered in Chapter 5.

The trust has the following benefits:

1. It requires family members to carefully analyze their desires regarding distribution of their estate.
2. It guarantees that probate can be avoided in its entirety, saving 5 to 10 percent of the estate and eliminating the usual delay of distribution from one to three years.
3. Because of the two preceding benefits, it minimizes the likelihood of friction within the family. Avarice among siblings is extremely common when a parent dies.
4. It can defer any payable taxation until both spouses have passed away.

5. An exemption is guaranteed when the second spouse dies of not less than $5 million as of 2012. This provides the potential for a substantially larger exemption if the surviving spouse continues ongoing planning and makes the appropriate elections. However, the present status of the legislation is such that the exemption will be reduced to $1 million effective January 1, 2013. Whether that will continue or be changed between the time this book is published and Congress decides to do some active labor, no one knows.

6. When the documents are prepared by competent drafters, all of the above can be accomplished with little likelihood of litigation. In situations where litigation does take place, there is low risk of a successful attack.

7. Used with a durable power of attorney for health care, it guarantees that health care needs can be immediately handled and assets can be managed efficiently if there is disability during the life of the individual and/or couple. This can be accomplished without a court controlled guardianship or conservatorship. (This benefit will be covered more thoroughly in Chapters 6 and 7.)

8. It allows the family to maintain total control over assets during the lifetime of the parents and the survivor of the spouses. It will also allow continued control within the family for a reasonable period of time.

9. It will in no way minimize the access of the family to its own wealth, even though a trust is a legal entity in the same way that a corporation is a legal entity.

10. When properly drafted, it maximizes family privacy during all periods of its existence—whether during the life of the creators of the trust, upon the death of those individuals, or during the life of subsequent beneficiaries.

It is absolutely critical to use competent drafters and technicians in the estate planning process. This does not include people who say you can accomplish quality estate planning with tear-out forms or those who write books and checklists without having adequate background or expertise in the kinds of analyses that are required, given the unique characteristics of every family.

Twenty-five years ago, this warning would not have been as meaningful. The profession was not faced with or prepared for the present extensive use of trusts in estate planning, and quality estate planners were difficult to find. Fortunately, this is no longer true. In virtually any area of the country, there are serious practitioners and competent advisors with the capacity to establish estate plans by using trusts.

It becomes mandatory that those professionals who have spent the time necessary to acquire the education and expertise are used to prepare quality trust documents. The sheer volume of documents as well as the current complexity of the tax laws, such as the incomprehensible problems of *generation-skipping transfer tax*, make this a must.

3

The Probate System

Problems with the Probate System

Problems with the probate system fall primarily into five categories:

1. Cost of probate
2. Time consumed in the probate process
3. Complexity of the system
4. The inherent uncertainty of the probate system
5. The practical loss of control by the family

Costs of Probate

There are two basic approaches in the United States to the charges under the probate system.

Historically, under probate codes, statutory fees were established and based on the size of the estate. However, in most instances, courts, as a matter of practice, have allowed additional fees commonly known as *extraordinary fees*.

As an example, statutory executor and attorney fees for one state (which is fairly representative of most states using this system) are shown in Illustration 3-1.

Illustration 3-1 Examples of Statutory Fees

California Statutory Probate Fees			
Probate Assets	Probate Fees	Probate Assets	Probate Fees
10,200	800	675,000	29,300
20,000	1,500	700,000	30,300
40,000	2,700	725,000	31,300
60,000	3,900	750,000	32,300
80,000	5,100	775,000	33,300
100,000	6,300	800,000	34,300
120,000	7,000	825,000	35,300
140,000	7,900	850,000	36,300
160,000	8,700	875,000	37,300
180,000	9,500	900,000	38,300
200,000	10,300	925,000	39,300
225,000	11,300	950,000	40,300
250,000	12,300	975,000	41,300
275,000	13,300	1,000,000	42,300
300,000	14,300	1,100,000	44,300
325,000	15,300	1,200,000	46,300
350,000	16,300	1,300,000	48,300
375,000	17,300	1,400,000	50,300
400,000	18,300	1,500,000	52,300
425,000	19,300	1,600,000	54,300
450,000	20,300	1,700,000	56,300
475,000	21,300	1,800,000	58,300
500,000	22,300	1,900,000	60,300
525,000	23,300	2,000,000	62,300

A more appropriate analysis of the cost of probate considers not only statutory fees for executors and attorneys, but also extraordinary fees, the cost of appraisals, accounting, court costs, and other miscellaneous expenses that are normally incurred. One of the more definitive studies that have been prepared on this subject, taking into consideration all administrative expenses, is shown in Illustration 3-2.[2]

---

[2] *See* GEORGE M. TURNER, REVOCABLE TRUSTS (5th ed, 2004).

Illustration 3-2 Table for Determination Probable Probate and Administrative Expenses*

Gross Estate Less Debts, Etc.		Probate and Administration Expenses**	
From (1)	To (2)	Amount on (1) (3)	Rate on Excess (4)
$ 0	$ 50,000	$ 0	8.6%
50,000	100,000	4,300	7.8%
100,000	200,000	8,200	7.2%
200,000	300,000	15,400	6.8%
300,000	400,000	22,200	6.5%
400,000	500,000	28,700	6.3%
500,000	600,000	35,000	6.0%
600,000	700,000	41,000	5.9%
700,000	800,000	46,900	5.8%
800,000	900,000	52,700	5.7%
900,000	1,000,000	58,400	5.6%
1,000,000	1,500,000	64,000	5.6%
1,500,000	2,000,000	92,000	5.6%
2,000,000	2,500,000	120,000	5.5%
2,500,000	3,000,000	147,500	5.5%
3,000,000	3,500,000	175,000	5.4%
3,500,000	4,000,000	202,000	5.3%
4,000,000	4,500,000	228,500	5.2%
4,500,000	5,000,000	254,500	5.1%
5,000,000	6,000,000	280,000	5.0%
6,000,000	7,000,000	330,000	4.9%
7,000,000	8,000,000	379,000	4.8%
8,000,000	9,000,000	427,000	4.7%
9,000,000	10,000,000	474,000	4.6%
10,000,000		520,000	4.5%***

* Actual expenses may vary greatly in the various jurisdictions. Where available, tables for local jurisdictions should be used.
** Includes attorneys', executors', accountants', and appraisers' fees, court fees, etc.
*** This rate will diminish somewhat as the size of the estate grows larger.

Some states are implementing a second approach for determining probate fees. Each case is analyzed on an individual basis, and the court determines the fees to be granted to executors and attorneys, based on the hours expended, the work accomplished, and the benefit to the estate.

Discussions with attorneys in other states suggest that there does not seem to be a significant difference in actual probate costs when this approach is used.

The probate costs shown in Illustration 3-2 on a $100,000 estate amount to $8,200 before any taxes are paid and before distributions are made to beneficiaries. Administration costs always come off the top. Illustration 3-3 shows the order in which the funds of the estate are dispersed.

Illustration 3-3 Order of Estate Payments and Distribution

1.	**Expenses**
2.	**Creditors**
3.	**Charitable Distributions, if any**
4.	**Estate Taxes**
5.	**Specific Gift, if any**
6.	**Beneficiaries** **Disposition of Residue**

On a $1 million estate, the average cost is about $64,000. In general, the amount of time, effort, and responsibility for a $1 million estate do not justify an expense that is eight times greater than the expense for a $100,000 estate.

Time of Probate

The time consumed by probate is a confusing issue—difficult to analyze under the best of circumstances. However, Illustration 3-4 may be helpful in examining the steps of a probate procedure and providing a reasonable time estimate. However, this illustration assumes no problems and total cooperation of family and courts. Both assumptions are probably fictional; eighteen to twenty-four months are more realistic.

Illustration 3-4

Probate Procedure	Time
A. File Petition to:	4–6 Weeks
1. Admit Will to Probate	
2. Appoint Executor	
B. File Notice to Creditor	4 Months
C. File Inventory and Appraisement	1 Week–1 Year
D. File Account and Order for Distribution	4–6 Weeks
E. File Receipts-Distribution	2–6 Weeks
F. File Closing Petition	4–6 Weeks
Total:	9–14 Months

Probate is simply a formal proceeding where a court takes authority and uses an executor or administrator over the assets of a person who has died. The proceeding involves many steps, hearings, analyses, and approvals.

Illustration 3-5 Complexity of Probate

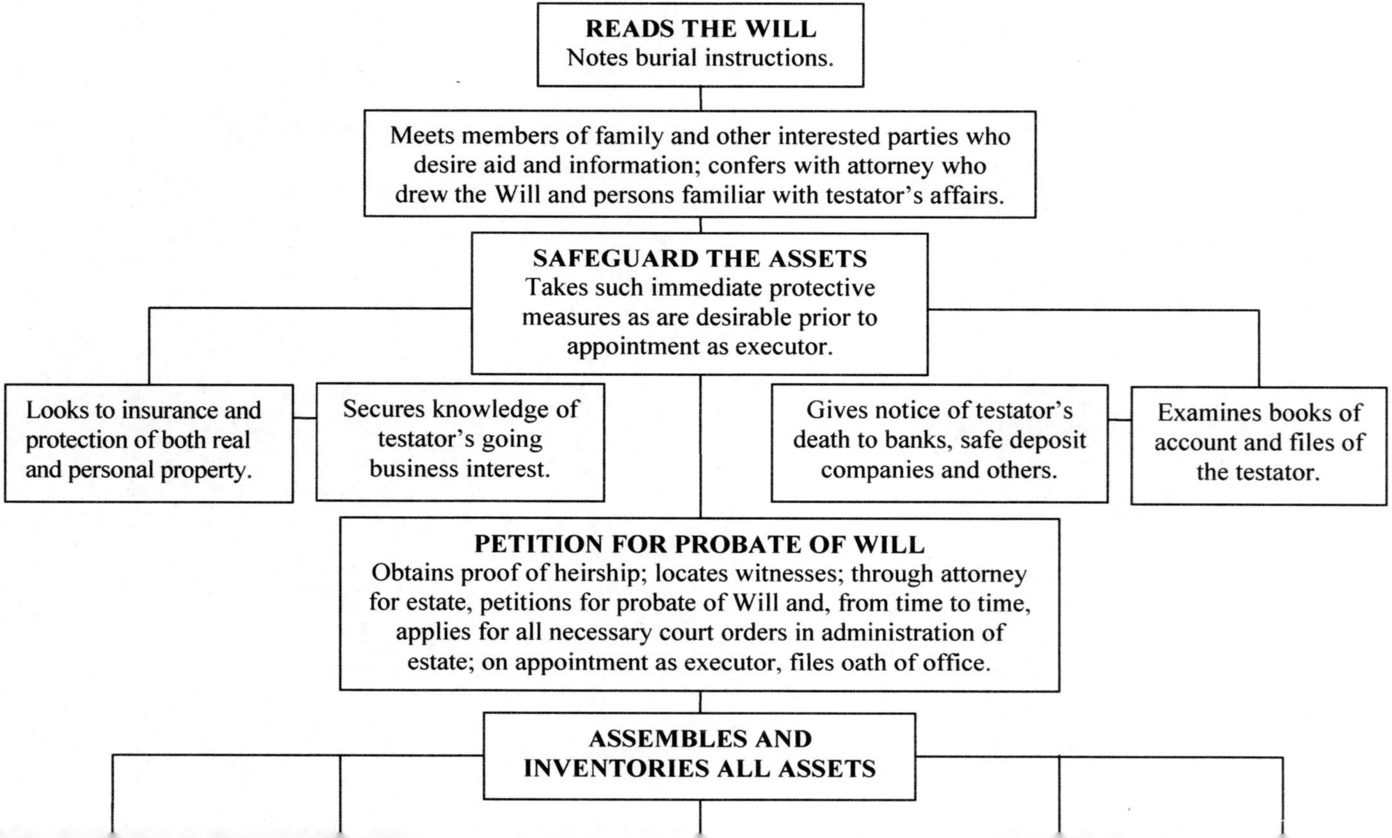

READS THE WILL
Notes burial instructions.

Meets members of family and other interested parties who desire aid and information; confers with attorney who drew the Will and persons familiar with testator's affairs.

SAFEGUARD THE ASSETS
Takes such immediate protective measures as are desirable prior to appointment as executor.

Examines books of account and files of the testator.

Gives notice of testator's death to banks, safe deposit companies and others.

Secures knowledge of testator's going business interest.

Looks to insurance and protection of both real and personal property.

PETITION FOR PROBATE OF WILL
Obtains proof of heirship; locates witnesses; through attorney for estate, petitions for probate of Will and, from time to time, applies for all necessary court orders in administration of estate; on appointment as executor, files oath of office.

ASSEMBLES AND INVENTORIES ALL ASSETS

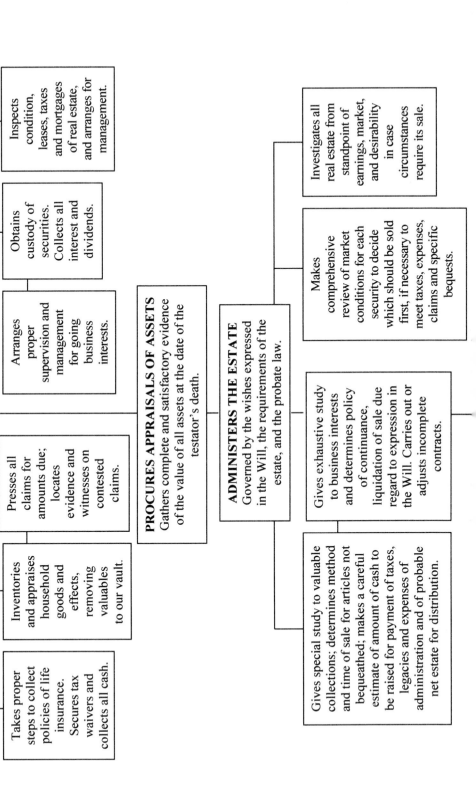

PROCURES APPRAISALS OF ASSETS
Gathers complete and satisfactory evidence of the value of all assets at the date of the testator's death.

- Inspects condition, leases, taxes and mortgages of real estate, and arranges for management.
- Obtains custody of securities. Collects all interest and dividends.
- Arranges proper supervision and management for going business interests.
- Presses all claims for amounts due; locates evidence and witnesses on contested claims.
- Inventories and appraises household goods and effects, removing valuables to our vault.
- Takes proper steps to collect policies of life insurance. Secures tax waivers and collects all cash.

ADMINISTERS THE ESTATE
Governed by the wishes expressed in the Will, the requirements of the estate, and the probate law.

- Investigates all real estate from standpoint of earnings, market, and desirability in case circumstances require its sale.
- Makes comprehensive review of market conditions for each security to decide which should be sold first, if necessary to meet taxes, expenses, claims and specific bequests.
- Gives exhaustive study to business interests and determines policy of continuance, liquidation of sale due regard to expression in the Will. Carries out or adjusts incomplete contracts.
- Gives special study to valuable collections; determines method and time of sale for articles not bequeathed; makes a careful estimate of amount of cash to be raised for payment of taxes, legacies and expenses of administration and of probable net estate for distribution.

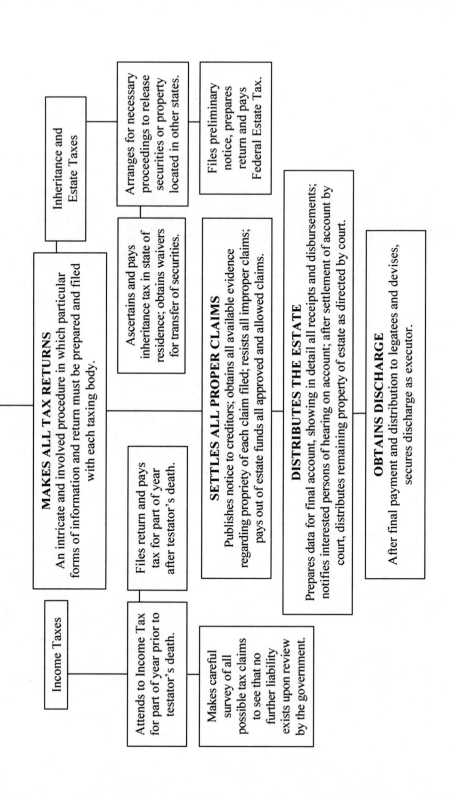

MAKES ALL TAX RETURNS
An intricate and involved procedure in which particular forms of information and return must be prepared and filed with each taxing body.

Income Taxes

Inheritance and Estate Taxes

Attends to Income Tax for part of year prior to testator's death.

Files return and pays tax for part of year after testator's death.

Ascertains and pays inheritance tax in state of residence; obtains waivers for transfer of securities.

Arranges for necessary proceedings to release securities or property located in other states.

Files preliminary notice, prepares return and pays Federal Estate Tax.

Makes careful survey of all possible tax claims to see that no further liability exists upon review by the government.

SETTLES ALL PROPER CLAIMS
Publishes notice to creditors; obtains all available evidence regarding propriety of each claim filed; resists all improper claims; pays out of estate funds all approved and allowed claims.

DISTRIBUTES THE ESTATE
Prepares data for final account, showing in detail all receipts and disbursements; notifies interested persons of hearing on account; after settlement of account by court, distributes remaining property of estate as directed by court.

OBTAINS DISCHARGE
After final payment and distribution to legatees and devises, secures discharge as executor.

When the organization published this illustration, the chart was criticized for making the system too complex. In an attempt to simplify the chart, they went back to the drawing board and came up with a new version of the same problem. This analysis is shown in Illustration 3-6.

Illustration 3-6 Administration of Estates in Probate

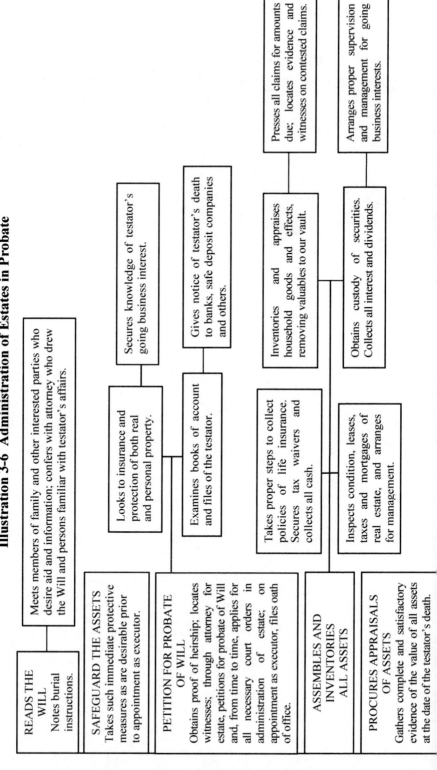

READS THE WILL
Notes burial instructions.

Meets members of family and other interested parties who desire aid and information; confers with attorney who drew the Will and persons familiar with testator's affairs.

SAFEGUARD THE ASSETS
Takes such immediate protective measures as are desirable prior to appointment as executor.

Looks to insurance and protection of both real and personal property.

Secures knowledge of testator's going business interest.

PETITION FOR PROBATE OF WILL
Obtains proof of heirship; locates witnesses; through attorney for estate, petitions for probate of Will and, from time to time, applies for all necessary court orders in administration of estate; on appointment as executor, files oath of office.

Examines books of account and files of the testator.

Gives notice of testator's death to banks, safe deposit companies and others.

ASSEMBLES AND INVENTORIES ALL ASSETS

Takes proper steps to collect policies of life insurance. Secures tax waivers and collects all cash.

Inventories and appraises household goods and effects, removing valuables to our vault.

Presses all claims for amounts due; locates evidence and witnesses on contested claims.

PROCURES APPRAISALS OF ASSETS
Gathers complete and satisfactory evidence of the value of all assets at the date of the testator's death.

Inspects condition, leases, taxes and mortgages of real estate, and arranges for management.

Obtains custody of securities. Collects all interest and dividends.

Arranges proper supervision and management for going business interests.

ADMINISTERS THE ESTATE

Governed by the wishes expressed in the Will, the requirements of the estate, and the probate law.

Makes comprehensive review of market conditions for each security to decide which should be sold first, if necessary to meet taxes, expenses, claims and specific bequests.

Investigates all real estate from standpoint of earnings, market, and desirability in case circumstances require its sale.

Gives special study to valuable collections; determines method and time of sale for articles not bequeathed; makes a careful estimate of amount of cash to be raised for payment of taxes, legacies and expenses of administration and of probable net estate for distribution.

Gives exhaustive study to business interests and determines policy of continuance, liquidation of sale due regard to expression in the Will. Carries out or adjusts incomplete

MAKES ALL TAX RETURNS

An intricate and involved procedure in which particular forms of information and return must be prepared and filed with each taxing body.

Income Taxes

Attends to Income Tax for part of year prior to testator's death.

Files return and pays tax for part of year after testator's death.

Makes careful survey of all possible tax claims to see that no further liability exists upon review by the government.

Inheritance and Estate Taxes

Arranges for necessary proceedings to release securities or property located in other states.

Files preliminary notice, prepares return and pays Federal Estate Tax.

Ascertains and pays inheritance tax in state of residence; obtains waivers for transfer of securities.

SETTLES ALL PROPER CLAIMS

Publishes notice to creditors; obtains all available evidence regarding propriety of each claim filed; resists all improper claims; pays out of estate funds all approved and allowed claims.

DISTRIBUTES THE ESTATE

Prepares data for final account showing in detail all receipts and disbursements; notifies interested persons of hearing on account; after settlement of account by court, distributes remaining property of estate as directed by court.

OBTAINS DISCHARGE

After final payment and distribution to legatees and devises, secures discharge as executor.

The entire system is so complex that it is not possible to draw a simple diagram of the probate process to give the public a complete or even a meaningful understanding of how it works.

Inherent Uncertainty of Probate

The complex and time-consuming procedures involved in the probate system tends to create uncertainty and tension within families and among the beneficiaries.

For instance, consider the death of my father, who left an estate of less than $15,000. On the day of the funeral, four of the children sat down and argued about which of them were going to receive the remainder of the estate upon the death of our mother.

Unfortunately, my experience is not unique. In more than forty-three years of practicing law, I have noticed that the tendency toward avarice among siblings rises to its highest level when a parent dies.

Sibling rivalries after the death of a parent are a constant for lawyers in the settlement of an estate. This problem is further compounded by the fact that family members cannot understand why it takes so long to settle an estate or why so much cost in fees are imposed on what they perceive to be their assets.

Many states have attempted to simplify their probate systems, but probate is still an inherently complex system with some insidious aspects. The only meaningful way to avoid the problem is to use a system with less complexity, lower cost, and more flexibility. The use of a revocable living trust, properly funded, will solve or minimize most of these problems.

4

Double Taxation

Overview

All families are allowed two basic types of exemptions. One exemption is commonly referred to as the *100 percent marital deduction*. This simply means that if a spouse dies and leaves the entire estate to the surviving spouse, all taxation is deferred until the death of the surviving spouse. Any taxation that might be imposed is determined by the size of the estate at that time.

The second exemption is the statutory exemption that has varied extensively over the years. For example, in 2001, it was $1 million per person. However, in 2011 and 2012, the exemption is $5 million per person. These are shown in Illustration 4-1.

This latter exemption was enacted in December 2010, and is known as the Tax Relief, Unemployment Insurance Reauthorization, and Job Creation Act of 2010. It was passed on December 16, 2010. However, it ends on December 31, 2012; hence, it leaves the planning process in a very difficult situation.

Illustration 4-1

Year	Top Tax Rate	Lifetime Exemption
2001	55%	$675,000
2002	50%	$1,000,000
2003	49%	$1,000,000
2004	48%	$1,500,000
2005	47%	$1,500,000
2006	46%	$2,000,000
2007	45%	$2,000,000
2008	45%	$2,000,000
2009	45%	$3,500,000
2010	0	0
2011	35%	$5,000,000
2012	35%	$5,000,000
2013	unknown	unknown

Losing the Exemption

Problems can arise when a spouse dies and all property is passed to the surviving spouse without using some type of trust system. For example, in Illustration 4-2, if the property simply goes from the couple to the surviving spouse on the death of the first of the spouses to die, then there will be imposed no taxation.

However, if, in the alternative, a double trust system is used, which is commonly referred to as an A-B trust system as shown in Illustration 4-3, then it is possible to minimize the taxation that will take place on the second death. The reason for this is that half of the estate or more, depending on the planning arrangement, will be allocated to the trust representing the first of the spouses to die. This is referred to as the decedent's trust, which is also technically referred to as the credit by-pass trust.

Any funds that are allocated in writing to the decedent's trust will be taxed, but the taxation on it will always be zero.

That amount will be held and distributed without taxation on the second death. It simply passes on to beneficiaries.

Obviously, depending on the size of the estate, this will eliminate a double taxation. If one simply passes it from the living spouse to the surviving spouse, then the exemption for the decedent spouse has been lost. In fact, if the surviving spouse died one month later, then both halves would be taxed against a double taxation.

A Caution on Larger Estates

Notwithstanding the benefits that the new law appears to allow for smaller and mid-size estates, the lack of benefits for larger estates is again included in the law.

Specifically, for those estates exceeding $10 million or greater at the time of death of an individual, there will be a decreasing tax credit or equivalent estate tax exemption that decreases until the estate reaches $20,040,000. The effect of this is that if the family is wealthy and the estate exceeds $20,040,000-plus, then functionally they have no credit or equivalent estate tax exemption.

Potential Disaster in 2013

After December 31, 2012, no one knows what will happen. Both Congress and the administration have been derelict and the public and estate planners are left incapable of accomplishing long-term planning.

Illustration 4-2 Problem of Double Taxation

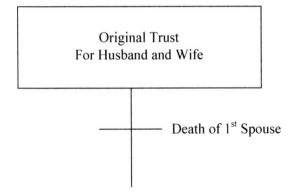

Original Trust
For Husband and Wife

Death of 1st Spouse

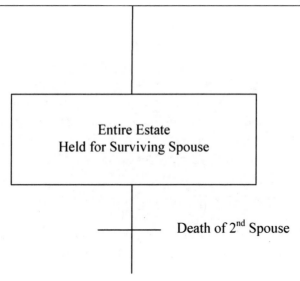

Entire Estate
Held for Surviving Spouse

Death of 2nd Spouse

Distribution to Beneficiaries

Illustration 4-3 Use of Double Trust System (A-B Trust)

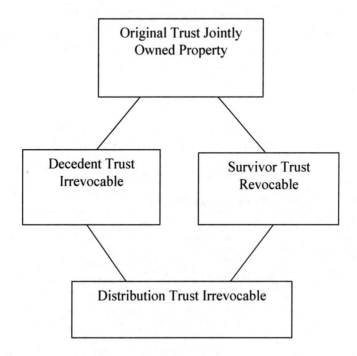

Original Trust Jointly
Owned Property

Decedent Trust
Irrevocable

Survivor Trust
Revocable

Distribution Trust Irrevocable

A Short-Term Trust Tax Benefit

If a double trust system is used, it is possible to retain the maximum exemption for both spouses in allowing for an exemption of a total of $10 million during the years 2011 and 2012.

Since the practical reality is that a husband and wife seldom die at the same time, and more realistic assumptions are that without a trust system, for every increase in exemption, that amount, plus interest, will be lost. The only organization that benefits from the failure to use a double trust (A-B Trust) is the Internal Revenue Service. As for this writer, they are not the favorite charity.

Possible Benefits and Ambiguities of the Tax Act of 2001

Illustration 4-4 shows the rates as they existed from the beginning of the year 2001 through the end of 2012.

The initial exemption in January 2001 was $675,000, but that amount was increased before the end of 2001, to $1 million per person.

Illustration 4-4 Combined Estate Tax Exemption and Top Tax Rates

Year	IRC § 2010 (c) Exemption	Maximum Tax Rate
2001	$675,000	55%
2002	$1,000,000	50%
2003	$1,000,000	49%
2004	$1,500,000	48%
2005	$1,500,000	47%
2006	$2,000,000	46%
2007	$2,000,000	45%
2008	$2,000,000	45%
2009	$3,500,000	45%
2010	0	0
2011	$5,000,000	35%
2012	$5,000,000	35%
2013	$1,000,000	55%

As you review the increase in exemptions beginning in 2001 and follow them through to the end of 2012, keep in mind that the laws that come into existence effective January 1, 2013, are simply unknown at the present time.

Given the fact that the new law may well end up terminating and/or minimizing the step-up in basis, except with a few situations, it appears that the best the present legislation can do is to be neutral. In all probability, over the next five to ten years, legislation will create a substantial increase in taxes imposed on the public by using different names and vehicles.

The election in Congress and the administration is not only unjustified, it is unconscionable in passing such a short-term law.

Families and tax advisors are simply left in a position where planning after December 31, 2012, is not currently a realistic possibility.

Changes in Capital Gains and Basis

Over the last twenty-five to thirty years, there have been significant increases and decreases in capital gains tax. It is one of those taxes where, depending on whether the powers in force in Washington will decide to either reward or punish the taxpayer, there is no way to reach a reasonable prognosis as to what direction they will take. However, common sense dictates that it could result in a very substantial tax increase, whether we call it death taxes, estate taxes, capital gains taxes, or gift taxes.

By way of simple example, at the present time it is generally acknowledged that 2 percent of citizens in the United States pay federal estate taxes. It would not be surprising if death taxes were repealed and the basis in the hands of the decedent individual passes on to the beneficiaries, that as many as 80 percent of the people in the United States would end up paying some form of capital gains and/or gift taxes. It does not take a genius to recognize the 2 percent, assuming even a minimum tax of 35 percent as compared to 80 percent as the probable lowest tax of 20 percent, will be providing an enormous increase in taxes payable to the federal government.

The effect of all of this confusion and ambiguity suggests that in the near term the best approach is to continue to use the basic decedent survivor's trust (A-B Trust), as it is the present practice among qualified estate planners. One of the useful characteristics of a revocable living trust is that as Congress modifies the ground rules, the citizenry may utilize amendments and/or termination of a trust altogether to ensure that the minimum amount of tax will be imposed on their estates.

It is a little discouraging that the way this has been presented by politicians has been to talk about the estate tax exemption, but never mentioning the fact that exemption does not continue on or does continue on after December 31, 2012. The ultimate conclusion is that one must approach this new legislation with serious reservations as to what characteristics it will have by the end of 2012 or early 2013.

5

Using the Revocable Living Trust

Trust Defined

An overview of the nature of a trust and diagrams illustrating how these trusts function provides the best understanding of the use of revocable living trusts.

The actual use of the revocable living trust is best understood through an overview of the nature of a trust and diagrams illustrating how these kinds of trusts function.

In its simplest form, a trust is an arrangement whereby a person holds property for the benefit of another. The person who creates a trust is usually known as the *trustor*. Trustors may also be known as *settlors* or *grantors*. The person who will receive the benefits of a trust is known as the *beneficiary*. The person who manages a trust is known as the *trustee*.

Another element of a trust has historically been known as a *res*. This simply means the *principal,* or *corpus,* of a trust, which includes any assets under the management of the trustee.

In many states, the trustor, trustee, and beneficiary may be the same person or persons. Unfortunately, historically some states such as New York, until recently, used an archaic analysis that, while technically accurate, is functionally meaningless. It states that the beneficiary cannot also act as the trustee. Perhaps this is simply a way of maintaining control over the estate for the banking and legal systems in that state. New legislation in New York may have corrected this impropriety. However, until tested, any new law is always suspected. With the level of consumer advocacy in the United States, it seems incredible that there are still states where a person cannot manage his or her own assets using a trust while acting as their own trustee.

This is not to suggest there is not a significant and useful role for trust companies, whose services can be invaluable when used properly. However, the practice of imposing institutional trustees upon the public, with no alternative manner of handling an estate, is indefensible. This statement is particularly true where many trust companies turn their collective noses up at estates under $2 million and many under $10 million. Those trust companies that see the economic value of servicing medium and even small estates are to be highly commended. Fortunately, some still serve the public.

Description of a Trust

Since trusts are so vital a tool to minimize taxes in the estate planning process, it is important to have a basic understanding of the elements of a trust and the unique way in which trusts function.

The four basic elements of a trust include:

1. *Trustor* (also referred to as settlor and grantor)—the individual(s) who brings the trust into existence;
2. *Trustee*—the manager of the trust;
3. *Beneficiary(s)*—those who are to receive the benefits of the trust as to either income or principal; and
4. *Res* (also referred to as corpus or principal)—the assets that are placed into the trust.

Trusts can be in any of four categories, which are:

1. A testamentary irrevocable trust;
2. A testamentary revocable trust (very rare);

3. A living revocable trust; and
4. A living irrevocable trust.

The first two types of trusts are brought into existence through a will, and the second two are brought into existence during lifetime, hence the terminology "living trust."

To understand trusts, you need to understand ownership of property prior to the existence of trusts and compare it to ownership of property under a trust as it developed.

Initially, an individual held property in his or her own name. This person had full use of the property and owned both legal title and *beneficial* title as demonstrated in Illustration 5-1. It began from the present and extended in theory to infinity.

Illustration 5-1 Diagram of a Fee Simple Absolute

LEGAL TITLE – Name on Asset Title
BENEFICIAL TITLE – Right to Exclusive Use of Assets

	∞
Present **Fee Simple Absolute (FSA)** **Infinity**	
(Sometimes referred to as a	
Fee Simple or Fee)	

This type of ownership is referred to as a *fee simple absolute*. This is still the basic way in which property is owned in those countries that derive their law from the historical common law. It is often referred to as a *fee simple* or a *fee*.

A trust, however, is an arrangement that divides the rights of legal ownership and beneficial ownership into two parallel levels, as demonstrated in Illustration 5-2.

Illustration 5-2 Diagram of the Basic Trust Concept

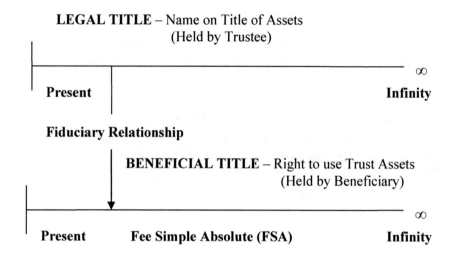

Historically, the individual or entity that owned legal title had to be different from the individual who had the right to use the property, or the beneficial owner. If both interests were held by the same individual or entity, it brought about a *"merger,"* and a trust no longer existed. Merger is no longer a problem except in a very few jurisdictions. In the vast majority of states, you can be both trustee and beneficiary.

The other distinct characteristic of a trust is that the relationship came into existence between the legal owner and the beneficial owner. This came to be known as *fiduciary responsibility*. In simple language, this meant that the responsibility was affirmatively imposed on the legal owner to use the property for the benefit of the equitable or beneficial owner, even if this use and treatment was detrimental to the legal owner.

Trust for a Single Person

Illustration 5-3 shows how a revocable living trust can be used for a single person—unmarried, divorced, or widowed. Mechanically, a person desiring to use a trust simply declares a trust into existence with a written document and may name himself or herself as trustee or manager, while retaining total power over the assets and continuing to be the sole beneficiary. In doing so, the trustor may also declare the document totally amendable and revocable.

Fortunately, the Internal Revenue Service no longer requires that a separate tax return be filed for any type of revocable trust. For all practical purposes, while an individual is living and not disabled, the procedure is that a trust is brought into existence, and the asset is changed from being held in the name of the individual to being held in the formal name of the trust.

The trust document should designate a successor trustee, if the original trustor dies or becomes disabled. Upon death, the trust arrangement becomes irrevocable or unchangeable by any person. The estate is then distributed in accordance with the provisions dictated by the person who established the trust.

Accompanying the revocable living trust instrument is a will, commonly known as a pour-over will. The reason for the name is that it is assumed all assets will be transferred into the trust during the lifetime of the person who established the trust. If this happens as intended, the pour-over will not be used. If, however, the assets need to be probated because they were not transferred to the trust during the trustor's lifetime, the purpose of the pour-over will is literally to pour over assets into the trust, which will eventually be distributed to the beneficiaries.

Use of the revocable living trust with the pour-over will builds the estate into a single arrangement to fully reflect the desires of the trustor (aka settlor/testator) and allows a maximum of privacy, a minimum of cost, and maintenance of appropriate dignity in the event of disability.

The value of this last feature can be best demonstrated by a personal experience of mine. About ten years ago, my sister suffered five strokes in four days. She was hospitalized for more than seven months, and, for a time, she suffered total disability. The strokes left her with an ongoing disability that will be with her for the rest of her life. Because she had a revocable trust that was fully funded with a durable power of attorney for health care (this will be discussed in Chapter 7), the person named was able to make decisions on her behalf. They were able to direct medical treatment immediately and to put the entire estate of her person and her wealth in proper order in less than two weeks.

In contrast, if such a representative had been required to go to probate court to have either a guardianship or a conservatorship imposed, the estate would have become nothing more than a living probate that could exist for the remainder of the patient's life. Further, it would have to be demonstrated that the patient was legally incompetent. This would be done through vivid testimony in open court and would include several examinations by the judge or appointee of the court. This system is inherently demeaning, expensive, inconsistent from case to case, and inefficient. My experience in just the first year is that the cost easily ranges from $7,000 to $12,000 and $3,000 to $6,000 in each subsequent year.

Given the reality that the average life expectancy is increasing steadily, and will continue to do so in the foreseeable future, probate courts will become progressively less efficient due to the sheer weight of numbers and the inherent inefficiency within the probate court system. These factors suggest the need for and advisability of increased use of revocable living trusts and durable power of attorney for health care.

Illustration 5-3 Single Trustor Trust

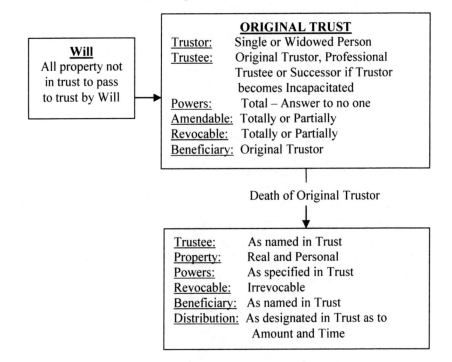

Revocable Living Trust with Pour-Over Will
for Single or Widowed Person

	ORIGINAL TRUST
Will All property not in trust to pass to trust by Will	Trustor: Single or Widowed Person
	Trustee: Original Trustor, Professional Trustee or Successor if Trustor becomes Incapacitated
	Powers: Total – Answer to no one
	Amendable: Totally or Partially
	Revocable: Totally or Partially
	Beneficiary: Original Trustor

Death of Original Trustor

Trustee:	As named in Trust
Property:	Real and Personal
Powers:	As specified in Trust
Revocable:	Irrevocable
Beneficiary:	As named in Trust
Distribution:	As designated in Trust as to Amount and Time

Revocable Trust for a Family

In a family situation, there is an additional benefit of a substantial tax savings when a revocable living trust is used. This was discussed to some extent in Chapters 3 and 4.

The initial or original trust is normally brought into existence by the declaration of both the husband and wife. There is no reason why the two cannot act together as co-trustees, except in the few states that prohibit this. A couple may continue to maintain absolute power over their estate and continue to be the sole beneficiaries of the acquired assets.

Illustration 5-4 Revocable Living Trust with Pour-Over Wills

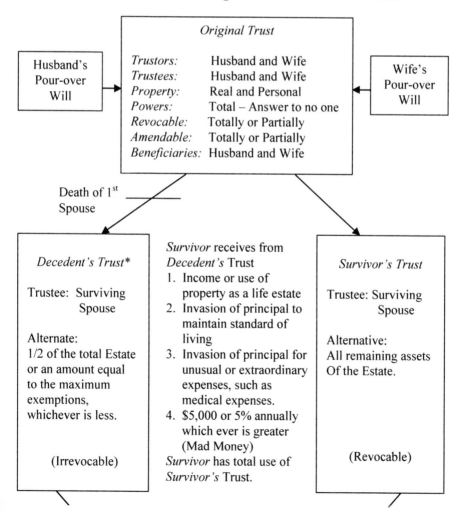

Death of 2nd
Spouse _____

```
┌─────────────────────────────────────┐
│          Children's Trust            │
│                                      │
│    Distribution as designated in Trust│
│          as to amount and time       │
│                                      │
│    Trustee:                          │
│                                      │
│            (Irrevocable)             │
└─────────────────────────────────────┘
```

In terms of sequence, the trust system can best be analyzed by three phases. Phase one is illustrated by the portion of the trust designated as the original trust. On the death of one of the spouses, the trust is divided into two trusts by the trustee, as demonstrated by Illustration 5-4(a).

Illustration 5-4(a) Phase One

```
┌──────────────────────────────────────────┐
│              Original Trust                │
│                                            │
│  Trustors:       Husband and Wife          │
│  Trustees:       Husband and Wife          │
│  Property:       Real and Personal         │
│  Powers:         Total – Answer to no one  │
│  Revocable:      Totally or Partially      │
│  Amendable:      Totally or Partially      │
│  Beneficiaries:  Husband and Wife          │
└──────────────────────────────────────────┘
```

During the life of the survivor, the survivor will have absolute and total right to all assets in the survivor's trust, including both income and principal. Since the arrangement is revocable, there is no limitation as to what the surviving spouse may do with those assets.

However, the survivor in this illustration is limited to four fundamental rights in terms of the decedent's trust. They are:

1. All income;
2. Use of the property;
3. Unusual and extraordinary expenses, such as medical bills; and
4. An annual invasion right of up to $5,000 or 5 percent, whichever is greater.

One may ask, "What is there under the decedent's trust that the survivor may not do?" From a practical standpoint, the only real prohibition is that the survivor does not have the right to give away assets in the decedent's trust or to waste those assets. Experience suggests that these are not real issues, except under unusual circumstances.

Experience also suggests that wives particularly like this approach, especially the provisions that take effect if they predecease their husbands. A term has been developed in the profession to describe the decedent's trust—*the anti-floozy trust*. The implication is that if the wife dies first, and the husband ends up meeting an opportunistic young woman, he will not have the right to give away the wife's interest in the estate. It will be preserved for their agreed-upon beneficiaries. Upon the death of the husband, the two estates will merge for the benefit of the children or whoever the designated beneficiaries may be, and not the new lady in his life. If the husband dies first, the decedent's trust is known as *the anti-gigolo trust* with all the same characteristics as *the anti-floozy trust*.

The four trusts—original trust, decedent's trust, survivor's trust, and children's trust—are included within the same legal document. Each of these trust arrangements comes into existence in phases. These phases do not overlap. They exist as independent periods of the trust's existence. The phases are summarized in Illustrations 5-4(a), 5-4(b) and 5-4(c).

With the death of one of the spouses, the original trust divides automatically into two trusts, as demonstrated by Illustration 5-4(b).

Illustration 5-4(b) Phase Two

Decedent's Trust*	Survivor receives from Decedent's Trust	Survivor's Trust
Trustee: Surviving Spouse	1. Income or use of property as a life estate	Trustee: Surviving Spouse
Alternate: 1/2 of the total Estate or an amount equal to the maximum exemptions, whichever is less.	2. Invasion of principal to maintain standard of living 3. Invasion of principal for unusual or extraordinary expenses, such as medical expenses. 4. $5,000 or 5% annually which ever is greater (Mad Money)	Alternative: All remaining assets of the Estate.
(Irrevocable)	Survivor has total use of Survivor's Trust.	(Revocable)

Illustration 5-4(c) Phase Three

Children's Trust
Distribution as designated in Trust as to amount and time
Trustee:
(Irrevocable)

Finally, pour-over wills are added to the system to ensure that any assets not transferred to the trust during a lifetime are poured into the trust at the death of either spouse.

The decedent's trust and the survivor's trust are sometimes referred to by other terms, such as *A/B trust, marital deduction trust, credit by-pass trust,* or other titles, which can be confusing. The decedent trust and survivor trust designations are appropriate and easy to understand. Decedent simply refers to the first spouse to die, and survivor refers to the surviving spouse. Unfortunately, the legal profession is all tied up in clever names, some of which are extremely technical, making them incomprehensible to the public.

Let us consider a total estate valued at less than $4 million in 2006. If one party dies, and half of the estate is attributable to the decedent's trust, and that trust is treated as irrevocable, the assets in that trust could be held as a life estate with reasonably broad invasion rights for the survivor. When the second spouse dies, the property in the trust representing the first of the two to die will not be subjected to death taxes, since it would have already been taxed. Therefore, the only amount that would be taxed is that which exceeded $2 million in the survivor's trust.

If the survivor can be convinced to use not only income, but also principal from the survivor's trust before consuming the principal of the decedent's trust, it will be possible to minimize the taxation on the second death.

A common variation of this trust is to use three trusts instead of two. A simple explanation of this approach is shown in Illustration 5-5.

Illustration 5-5

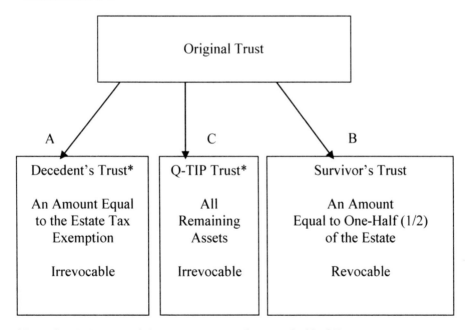

*Decedent's Trust and Q-TIP Trust equal to one-half of Estate

This trust arrangement ensures that half of the trust assets are retained for the benefit of the persons chosen as beneficiaries by the first spouse to die. Normally, this is accomplished by using the decedent's trust, which protects the tax exemption for the first spouse to die.

Then, half of the total estate goes into the survivor's trust, and any property that exceeds the tax exemption in the decedent's trust is placed into a qualified terminal interest property trust, or simply the Q-TIP trust.

The Q-TIP trust has the same characteristics as a decedent's trust in that it allows the survivor the use of income and principal to maintain a normal standard of living for the survivor. However, the survivor will only be able to have absolute control over half of the estate—that is, those assets allocated to the survivor's trust. The reason for this is that, for functional purposes, the survivor's trust is revocable and amendable. Hence, the survivor can do as he or she deems appropriate with that portion of the estate. Assets held in the decedent's trust and/or decedent's trust and Q-TIP trust will allow the survivor to have income and principal to maintain the standard of living plus a potential maximum of 5 percent mad money under the decedent's trust, but the distribution of those assets at the death of the survivor will go to those individuals who were named during the time that both spouses were alive. Hence, the principal not utilized in either the decedent's trust or the Q-TIP trust will go to the beneficiaries as was desired by the decedent.

A similar, but more secure result can be accomplished by means of a contract between the husband and wife called a third-party beneficiary contract. In this arrangement, the spouses covenant that, upon the death of one party, the survivor will make no fundamental changes in distributions to beneficiaries in either amount or time in the survivor's trust. These contracts are extremely useful, in that they can provide a maximum amount of comfort to spouses who are concerned about the estate being dissipated after their demise or not being distributed to the beneficiaries that they desire. It leaves the floozy and gigolo out in the cold.

The use of a third-party beneficiary contract can be very sophisticated. This again dictates the need for the use of knowledgeable counsel to ensure that the desires of both parties are adequately addressed.

The Non-Traditional Family

The double trust system (as shown in Illustration 5-6) may also be used by the non-traditional family as well as by a single individual or a family in the traditional sense. A non-traditional family can be a man and woman living together without the benefit of matrimony, or two people of the same gender living together and planning to share their estates.

The same benefits of the preservation of the $2 million exemption in 2006 and the elimination of probate and conservatorships can be accomplished simply by changing the titles or names of the persons involved. For example, instead of referring to the husband and wife, the trust document may refer to the participants by their actual names.

This is an area where a trust arrangement should have significant appeal, since those living in non-traditional families often desire privacy and are concerned about how their assets will be handled. This proves true to an even greater extent than with a traditional family. For further details on the non-traditional family, see Chapter 10.

Illustration 5-6 Trust for a Couple of Same Gender

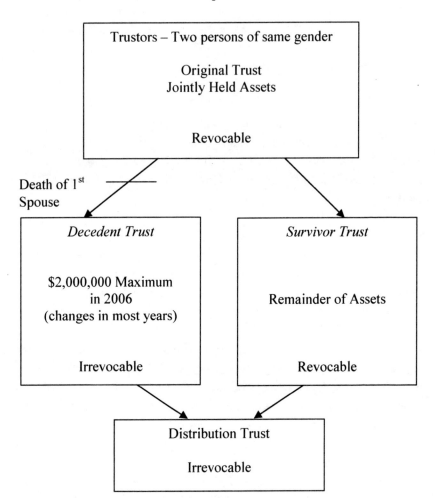

Trustors – Two persons of same gender

Original Trust
Jointly Held Assets

Revocable

Death of 1st Spouse

Decedent Trust

$2,000,000 Maximum
in 2006
(changes in most years)

Irrevocable

Survivor Trust

Remainder of Assets

Revocable

Distribution Trust

Irrevocable

Benefits of a Trust for the Single Person

Introduction

There are three basic benefits for the single, widowed, or divorced individual in using a revocable living trust. They are:

1. Avoidance of probate;
2. Care of the individual in case of physical, mental, or emotional disability; and
3. The segregation of assets in the event of a new marriage to avoid commingling of funds, which may compromise an individual's right to his or her own property.

Avoidance of Probate

As described in Chapter 3, the revocable living trust allows all of the benefits for a single person that are provided for a family, with the exception of the deferral of taxation of the estate until the second person's death, as explained in Chapter 4. Any death taxes required will be due and payable within nine months after the death of the single person. The other benefits that have been previously discussed, including reasonable privacy and reduction of time and cost in the settlement of probate, are fully available for a single individual.

Also, by establishing a revocable living trust, the single person will not, in any way, give up control or access to his or her assets. The single individual, acting as the trustor or creator of the trust, as trustee or manager

and/or as sole beneficiary of the trust, has absolute and total
ver all assets of the trust. The individual can engage in any type of
ction he or she might desire, regardless of how risky it may be.

Care of the Individual in Cases of Physical, Mental, or Emotional Disability

The benefit of using a trust for a single person may best be illustrated again by my sister, who survived a serious illness. During a four-day period, this middle-aged widow suffered five extremely debilitating strokes. She required hospitalization in various care facilities, ranging from intensive care to a rehabilitation center, for about eighteen months.

She had a revocable living trust, fully funded with all of her assets and a durable power of attorney for health care. Because her estate planning was in order, it was possible for me to take control of her assets and manage all of her affairs during the disability period without any intrusion of the court system. Also avoided was the necessity for the demeaning process of having her appear in open court with the accompanying delays, inefficiencies, expense, and personal embarrassment.

In fact, just the opposite occurred. Within two days of the actual diagnosis, her affairs were under my control. Furthermore, over the next two years, the integrity of her estate was maintained, and her personal dignity was fully preserved. In contrast, without a revocable living trust and durable power of attorney for health care, we would have had to file for conservatorship for her person and her estate. This would have required publication time, court appearances, and delays. Years later, when we discussed the benefits, even she was surprised at the value of the system we implemented and was deeply grateful.

The Segregation of Assets in the Event of a New Marriage to Avoid Commingling

In our society, divorce is common, and the premature death of a spouse is always a possibility. The revocable living trust acts as a unique vehicle to segregate the assets of those entering into second marriages in situations where one's assets were acquired prior to marriage. For instance, a husband and wife in their fifties, who may subsequently be divorced or widowed, may have acquired substantial personal assets before entering the second marriage.

The parties may want to maintain the value of those assets and prohibit the claim of the other to access each party's assets or inheritance. What options are available to facilitate this? Prenuptial and postnuptial agreements have not proved to be completely effective. For reasons that are not completely clear, there seems to be a preconceived idea in the courts that such agreements should be treated with disdain, and they are often functionally invalidated by the courts, regardless of the intent of the parties at the time the agreement was adopted.

What is needed is a system where there can be a clear segregation of assets, leaving no question as to which assets are the sole and separate property of either spouse, and what property should be categorized as property acquired by the effort of the couple during the marriage.

Although common law states and community property states use different language, it appears that, for all practical purposes, most states treat property of individuals after death or divorce in the same way.

First, it appears that most jurisdictions do not look with great favor on prenuptial or postnuptial agreements alone, since it is too easy for the property to be commingled or for the parties to act in a way that makes tracing the original source impossible or extremely difficult. Therefore, a triple trust system may currently be the best answer.

This system includes using a sole and separate property trust for both the man and the woman (two of the three trusts). The documentation would clearly show that all property within the trusts was to be treated as sole and separate property, and that no person, other than named beneficiaries, have any present right to it, nor any rights to receive inheritance of that property.

The third trust would be a trust for those assets acquired during the marriage, which would be treated under the laws of the particular jurisdiction governing assets acquired through the effort of either spouse after the marriage took place.

Attempts are sometimes made through prenuptial agreements to allow for earnings to be maintained separately in the event of the death of one of the spouses. This techniques leads to an uphill fight in any court battle. The validity of such an agreement is often successfully challenged. However, if there is a carefully drawn prenuptial or postnuptial agreement, with *both* parties represented by independent counsel, and if the triple trust system described above is used, it would be possible for the individuals to maintain the separate nature of their own assets. The three trusts should be clearly defined and incorporated as an integral aspect of a prenuptial or postnuptial agreement.

Illustration 6-1 demonstrates graphically how this arrangement could work when both spouses desire to have their separate property go to someone other than the surviving spouse after their death.

Illustration 6-1   Estate Planning for Families with Jointly Owned Property and Sole and Separate Property

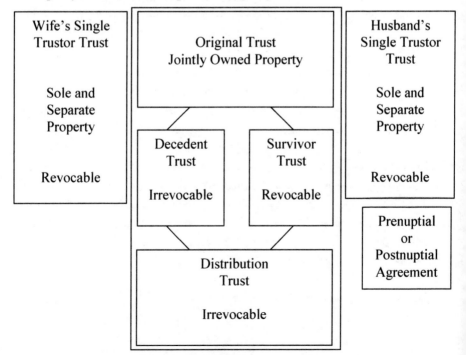

Experience over the years in using this type of multiple trust—from small estates to large estates with assets in the millions—has been extremely positive. So far, no court challenge to the use of this arrangement has been successful. However, in every case, separate competent counsel have represented each party.

7

Elements and Documents
of a Quality Estate Plan

Introduction

If a quality estate plan is to be prepared for anyone, regardless of the size of the estate, the following documents ought to be considered fundamental:

1. Family revocable living trust for couples, single individuals, and non-traditional couples;
2. Accompanying pour-over wills;
3. Powers of attorney for health care;
4. Living will declarations;
5. Burial or cremation directives;
6. Declaration regarding status and character of properties;
7. Necessary transfer documents to ensure that assets are transferred to the revocable living trust; and
8. Powers of attorney for asset management for some, but not all.

As the estate grows larger and/or more complicated, then the following documents should also be considered:

1. Individual revocable trusts for each spouse;
2. IRC 2503(c) children's trust (for children under twenty-one years of age);[3]

---

[3] I.R.C. §2503(c) (1998).

3. IRC 2503(b) children's trust (for children over twenty-one years of age);[4]
4. Crummey trust (for gifting and insurance);
5. Irrevocable creditor protection trusts;
6. Declarations regarding domicile;
7. Holographic will for personal items;
8. Family limited partnerships or limited liability companies;
9. Charitable foundations; and
10. Charitable trusts of various kinds.

The sole purpose of this chapter is to suggest the necessary documents and to provide a succinct statement describing the benefit of each document. For a total list of documents to consider for a quality estate plan for a family, see Illustration 7-1.

Illustration 7-1

**Approaches and Documents to Consider in
Establishing a Complete Quality Estate Plan**

1. Family revocable living trust
2. Accompanying pour-over wills
3. Powers of attorney for health care
4. Living will declarations
5. Burial directives
6. Declaration regarding status and character or properties
7. Necessary transfer documents to ensure that assets are transferred to the trustee of the trust agreement
8. Individual revocable trusts for each spouse
9. IRC 2503 children's trusts[5]
10. Crummey insurance trusts
11. Irrevocable creditor protection trusts
12. Declarations regarding domicile
13. Holographic will for personal items
14. Family limited partnerships or limited liabilities

---

[4] *Id.* §2503(b).
[5] *Id.* §2503.

Revocable Living Trust between Husband and Wife

When a husband and wife use a revocable living trust, they are seeking assurance that all taxes will be deferred until both parties have died and that there will be a minimum exemption on the second death of $5 million or more under the current tax laws. Depending on the method used to divide the estate after the first death, it may be possible to increase the functional exemption substantially.

The trust arrangement also provides for maximum privacy and for minimum risk of litigation by individuals who believe they have some claim against the estate (see Chapter 5). Experience demonstrates that the fewer people involved in the settlement of an estate, the more efficient and less expensive the settlement process becomes.

Through use of the revocable living trust, the number of individuals can be limited to the trustee plus legal investments and accounting advisors. The surviving spouse may desire additional information from others, such as a financial planner or insurance agent. Under some circumstances, it may also be necessary to use probate courts.

Compared to the cumbersome procedures that result from the use of a will, the entire process of administering an estate using a trust can be reduced to four minimum steps:

1. Preparing an inventory of the estate assets;
2. Appraising the assets of the estate;
3. Preparing tax returns and paying taxes, if any; and
4. Making distributions in accordance with the terms of the trust.

An examination of the probate procedure, as shown in Illustrations 3-5 and 3-6 in Chapter 3, demonstrates the great difference between the two systems. This assumes the trust has been properly funded.

In addition, if both spouses become disabled, or the surviving spouse becomes disabled, a trust system provides a way to reduce or eliminate the need for a guardianship or conservatorship, depending on the nature of the assets and the particular situation. Without the use of some kind of trust, there is no meaningful way to protect the economic and personal rights of the disabled owner of the property.

Revocable Living Trust for a Single Individual

For the single individual, the revocable living trust provides the advantage that the estate will not be probated, provided it is properly funded with the individual's assets. Therefore, less time and cost is involved than with any other system. There is also assurance of maximum privacy. The need for a conservatorship or guardianship in the event of incapacity could also be eliminated.

Pour-Over Wills

When the family or individual has not transferred all assets to the trust, the pour-over will transfers assets through probate into the trust, so they can be distributed according to the trust provisions.

There is potential for probate on any assets not transferred to the trust. If all of the assets have been appropriately transferred to the trust, the necessity for actually probating the pour-over will is eliminated.

In a sense, it is a "just in case" document. However, in some jurisdictions, there may be reason to consider probating some assets in the event of a potential creditor issue. The filing of probate imposes statutes of limitations of three to six months, depending on the state. If there are minor children, the pour-over will also functions as the only vehicle through which a guardian of minor children can be named.

Failure to use the pour-over will with a revocable living trust may create unbelievable havoc in the estate-settlement process. If some assets are not in the trust, the laws of intestacy in the particular state may dictate that the assets go to different beneficiaries than those designated in the trust document. Only assets that are placed in the trust during an individual's lifetime or are transferred to the trust through the accompanying pour-over will can be distributed to the desired beneficiary.

Power of Attorney for Health Care

When an individual becomes incapacitated physically, mentally, or emotionally, and cannot direct his or her own health care needs, there are only two ways these needs can be accomplished. The traditional way is to name someone under a conservatorship or guardianship arrangement, which is functionally nothing more than a living probate. The Probate Court takes jurisdiction over the individual's assets during the disability. For all practical purposes, all of the inherent difficulties that have been described with the probate procedure come into play.

The second method, the power of attorney for health care, is a private method, authorized in most states, that allows a person to give another person (along with alternates) full authority in the event of disability. This person can direct hospitals, doctors, and others to provide health care appropriate to the person's circumstances at the time.

The power of attorney for health care has been demonstrated to be effective, while keeping the administrative problems associated with implementing a court-controlled program to a minimum. Accordingly, there is a reduction in cost compared to the court system for conservatorship appointments. Obviously, it is critical that persons chosen to serve as guardians and/or conservators with authority over medical services have good judgment and integrity, and be without dishonorable motives.

Living Will Declaration
(aka Directive to Physician or Do Not Resuscitate)

Most states now permit the use of living will declarations (directive to physicians). This is an arrangement for individuals whose health has deteriorated to the point where there is no realistic likelihood of conscious living without extreme life support. With the concurrence of two doctors, life support systems, such as respiration devices, can be removed, and the individual is allowed to die with dignity. In fact, some states have actually titled their legislation, The Right to Die in Dignity.

It is critical that this argument for a living will declaration not be confused with the questionable arguments being raised regarding euthanasia or the arguments of people who simply do not want to live. This is *not* a Kevorkian document. Those arguments are entirely different in nature and quality and have not yet been thoroughly analyzed by the public or by legislative bodies throughout the United States.

The living will declaration applies only when a person has reached a state where the continuation of life support would be little more than the preservation of a "living" cadaver.

Burial Directive or Cremation Directive

It has become increasingly desirable for people to indicate how they want their remains to be handled. Some people prefer to be buried in a particular area or with a family member in a particular location, or want services to be conducted in specific ways.

Cremation is gaining popularity. Because of some serious abuses, failure to use a cremation directive, a requirement for court approval has become progressively more common.

Many states have now adopted legislation that allows an individual to make such a burial or cremation directive, and the legislation in some cases even provides for criminal penalties to be imposed for non-compliance with the wishes of the deceased.

Historically, it has not been uncommon to state such desires in a will. Although that may work, it is not near as efficient and cost effective as a formal Burial or Cremation Directive.

Declaration Regarding Status of Property

Many states distinguish property acquired during marriage from property received by gift or by testamentary documents. It is important that the relationship and ownership rights of such property be clearly delineated.

Otherwise, significant legal issues may arise concerning taxation and inheritance rights to such properties.

Under certain circumstances, the size or nature of assets that are clearly owned totally by one spouse may be sufficient reason to segregate those assets into a separate trust. This will maximize the individual's ability to maintain the integrity of the interest that he or she has in the property.

In community property states, this may be particularly true. The basic premise of community property law is that all property owned by spouses during the period of the marriage is considered community property—that is, each spouse owns an undivided one-half interest of all assets. This is a rebuttable presumption, and therefore, if the integrity of some asset or assets is clearly demonstrated to be the sole and separate property of an individual living in a community property state, documentation to that effect becomes progressively critical in establishing the proper status.

For this reason, if none other, all assets need to be clearly described to counsel, along with their nature, origin, and believed ownership rights. In this way, proper analysis and documentation can be provided to protect the interests of everyone involved. This is one of the least understood problems in the estate-planning process. It is commonly and grossly overlooked, which results in more litigation and strife among family members.

The Use of a Trust to Minimize Taxation of Life Insurance

The taxation of life insurance may be one of the most complex issues in the US tax system for two reasons. First, the Internal Revenue Service appears to go to great lengths to tax insurance proceeds. Second, the case law over many years has been diverse and inconsistent concerning the concept of *"incidents of ownership."* Unless careful planning is undertaken with counsel, financial planners, and underwriters who understand their subject, it is highly probable that life insurance will be taxed at the time of death of the insured.

In fact, experience in more than forty-three years of legal practice shows that in 90 percent plus of cases, because of the way the policy was applied for, owned, or paid for, the proceeds have been included in an individual's estate, and death taxes are imposed, even when this result was clearly not intended. This one area of the law appears to be more important than substance or intent.

Part of the problem is the insurance industry's tragic lack of understanding of the taxation system. For example, some of the bulletins that have been received from eastern insurance companies concerning community property state law are not only pathetic and inaccurate, but border on malpractice. It is amazing that more litigation has not been brought against insurance companies for their failure to research this subject more thoroughly and to provide proper education to their field forces and administrative personnel on the subject. Also, the fact that the three-year contemplation of death statute* is still applicable to life insurance products makes it even more important that careful analysis be made of how life insurance should be purchased, administered, and taxed.

An irrevocable trust created by the proper individual, funded in a way that complies with the law—with careful and consistent reporting in accordance with the Internal Revenue Code, Treasury regulations, and court interpretations—maximizes the possibility that life insurance proceeds will not be included in the individual's estate. In fact, irrevocable trusts are the most effective vehicle for isolating life insurance to keep it from being included in an individual's estate (see details in Chapter 14).

Unfortunately, there are many strange types of irrevocable trusts used for this purpose, which have been declared illegal or have been so narrowly defined by courts that they are unusable. It is my opinion that the so-called "super trust" of the 1970s has long gone by the boards. The so-called *Crummey* trust is a viable instrument, if properly drafted and carefully administered.** However, getting clients to give proper notice *every* time appears close to impossible.

Using irrevocable trusts under Section 2503(c) or Section 2503(b) of the Internal Revenue Code may be the most effective technique to ensure that estates are protected against the imposition of death taxes on life insurance proceeds.[6] This strategy is further discussed in Chapter 14. In the area of *buy-sell agreements,* where there are three or more individuals, it may be that an irrevocable trust is the ideal way to arrange the life insurance policy for the buy-out of a deceased partner or stockholder.

* This is congressional legislation that provides that all gifts for three years prior to death are treated as date of death gifts.
** The Crummey trust requires that all beneficiaries be noticed annually and given an opportunity to withdraw gifting from prior year.

Transferring of Assets to the Trust

Essential to preparing estate-planning documents is clear and precise information that shows the exact mechanics to be employed in transferring assets to the trust. For example, the transfer of a couple's residence into a trust is usually best handled by legal counsel. The property must be transferred from the name of the husband and wife as individuals to the name of the husband and wife as co-trustees, with an appropriate designation of the existence and date of the trust.

A well-established trust name used successfully for years is as follows:

> Thomas O. More and Jane C. More, Co-Trustees,
> U/D/T dated September 2, 2005,
> F/B/O The More Family

The designation "U/D/T" means "Under Declaration of Trust." The designation "F/B/O" means "For the Benefit of."

In contrast, individuals must usually assume the responsibility of transferring stock and bond accounts with a brokerage firm by personally providing the brokerage firm with a certification of trust (with relevant pages attached from the trust) transferring either individual stock certificates or the stock account to the name of the trust. Many brokerage firms now provide clients with a preprinted certification form.

---

[6] I.R.C. §§2503(b)-(c).

To help ensure that you transfer assets properly, legal counsel should provide a detailed letter of instruction providing the name of the trust and the method by which all types of assets should be transferred to the trust.

Irrevocable Creditor Protection Trust

For those who are engaged in the types of businesses that make creditor protection critical, it may be useful to establish an irrevocable trust in which gifts are made to either a spouse and/or children on an irrevocable basis. In doing this, there may be a sacrifice of other types of gifting that might otherwise be useful through other kinds of trusts such as a Section 2503(c) children's trust.[7]

However, where creditor protection is at issue, such trusts vary greatly in form and kind, from a simple common law trust, to irrevocable trusts with incomplete gifts for tax purposes, to the very complicated use of Massachusetts business trusts.

The very complexity of the issues involved in creditor protection again demonstrates the need for the public to seek out and utilize competent attorneys who are experienced in this area of the law.

Declaration Regarding Domicile

Because the US Supreme Court has never settled the issue of the possibility of dual domicile by an individual or a family, it may be necessary and appropriate to clearly define the claimed domicile through a formal declaration.

In doing this, there should be recitals of location of the residents, the fact that voting is limited to the one state, that state taxes are being paid in that state, as well as other relevant issues that counsel can assist in including in such a declaration. Practical experience in using these documents over a significant period demonstrates that in every incidence thus far, it has eliminated the issue of arguments about duel domicile.

---

[7] §2503(c).

Holographic Will

A holographic will is a document that normally has the characteristics of being wholly written in the handwriting of the testator, dated by the testator, and signed by the testator. It is usually a document that has no other printing and/or writing or attestation of witnesses, or notarization.

States vary significantly in the way in which holographic wills are treated as legally binding and, therefore, these should be considered dangerous.

This does not mean they should not be used. It simply means that individual counsel should carefully explain both verbally and in writing the methods that should be employed for a valid holographic will to be utilized.

From a practical standpoint, I recommend that holographic wills be limited to those situations where the individual desires to gift personal items that are not of significant financial value to individuals or family members. If the item has significant financial value, it is recommended that it be included as a specific gift under either a will, or preferably a trust.

Family Limited Partnerships

As long as family limited partnerships carefully follow the law in the state of the domicile of the family and are not intended to be a financial ruse, this is found to be an extremely useful vehicle.

I have gone through numerous audits where family limited partnerships have been challenged and/or at least audited. It is found that, as long as reasonable limits are used in the gifting process, drafting is appropriately handled, and tax returns are filed on a regular basis, the Internal Revenue Service has looked upon them with significant favor. On the other hand, in those situations where there has been obvious and significant abuse, the Internal Revenue Service can become a very formidable enemy in the attempted use of a family limited partnership. However, it should be pointed out that any fictional person such as a partnership or corporation when inappropriately used for other than the purpose that legislation brought the entity into existence, are always subject to serious attack by taxing agencies.

Because of progressive abuses of the family limited partnership, the use of the less tainted limited liability company may be preferable.

Charitable Giving Through Foundations and Charitable Trust

The use of charitable vehicles has been lumped under one heading. The purpose for this is that the complexity of charitable giving in various forms of charitable remainder trusts, a charitable lead trust, etc., is so complicated. To attempt in a guide of this size to provide meaningful explanation could not possibly do the subject justice.

This is a classic example of where mature, experienced, and competent legal counsel should be sought in the analysis, preparation, and usability of any of these vehicles for all persons or families.

However, by way of example, a commonly used charitable vehicle is a charitable remainder annuity trust. This is a vehicle where an asset of some kind is gifted to a charitable trust. The trustee in turn makes an annual payment of not less than 5 percent of the value to the grantor of the gift during their lifetime. Upon the death of the beneficiaries of the trust, the principal asset(s) of the trust is then delivered free of trust to the charitable institution. In many cases, this is found to be a very secure way to provide an ongoing annuity payment.

However, three elements should always be kept in mind. The Internal Revenue Service is looking very closely at denotative intent. What this means is that there should be some relationship between the maker of the gift and the charity to whom it is being given. Transactions through the use of charitable vehicles that are done for tax purposes only commonly end up creating an expensive fiasco.

The second is that the institutional trustee that is going to be responsible in managing the trust and making distributions should have a proven track record. Many charitable trusts have become insolvent with the individual families being left without the charitable institution having the ability to make payments.

The third element involved in this problem is one of valuating assets that are being transferred to some form of charitable trust. Historically, there have been many cases where assets have been grossly overvalued, and both the family and the charity have suffered by the failure to be realistic about valuation.

8

Federal Estate Tax for the Non-United States Citizen

Legislation

Almost literally in the middle of the night, in November of 1988, the US Congress passed legislation that adversely affected the tax exemptions available to non-citizen residents of the United States as well as non-resident citizens. Specifically, the law provides that 100 percent of marital deductions are not allowed for property passed from an individual who has died to the surviving spouse if the surviving spouse is a non-citizen, and that property is to be received outright, or if it was in a trust wherein the non-citizen spouse acted as the sole trustee.

Marital Deduction

The impact of this legislation can be understood best by first recognizing the nature of the 100 percent marital deduction. The deduction means that when a spouse dies and leaves assets outright to the surviving spouse, there is a 100 percent deduction. Therefore, the amount of taxes due to the US government would be zero.

Fortunately, however, the government has provided a method by which full use of the 100 percent marital deduction can be also made available to non-citizens.

This is accomplished by using a trust wherein the property is transferred for the benefit of the resident non-citizen, using a trustee who is either a

US citizen or a US trust company, or a combination of the two. Where a co-trusteeship is used, the non-citizen may serve as a trustee with a US citizen or a US trust company. Under this circumstance, the 100 percent marital deduction becomes available.

The number of non-citizens living in the United States is literally in the millions. While good for the Internal Revenue Service, the impact of this legislation can be devastating unless proper estate-planning documents have been prepared.

There is nothing in the legislation to indicate that the $675,000 to $1 million estate tax equivalent exemption, as discussed in Chapter 4, has been nullified. All writings on the subject would suggest that the exemption is still available, even in the situation where property is passed to a non-citizen resident or to a non-citizen, per se. The initial trust representing a husband and wife, regardless of their citizenship, could be established so that both parties are acting as co-trustees. However, upon the death of one of the parties, if the surviving spouse is a resident non-citizen, the trusteeship provision must provide that either a US citizen acts as the trustee or the trust representing the interest of the decedent has a co-trusteeship involving a US citizen and/or a US trust institution, and the surviving spouse. If the non-US citizen dismisses the United States citizen or US trust company, it could be a fatal flaw in prevention of a double taxation of the estate.

It seems this legislation was purely intended to ensure that the US government was receiving taxes from individuals who might otherwise leave the country without paying appropriate death taxes.

An Example

If an estate is worth $2 million, and one spouse died in 1997 leaving a resident non-citizen as the survivor, the taxation of the estate would be as follows:

Gross Estate:	$5,000,000
Less equivalent estate tax exemption:	$ 600,000

Taxable estate: $1,400,000
Total tax due and payable
within nine months: $ 512,800

This example does not take into consideration any deductions for expenses. It also does not take into consideration the increasing equivalent estate tax exemption, which will be $1 million in 2001 and increased to $1.5 million, then to $3.5 million in 2009, and to $5 million in 2011 and 2012 per person.

In contrast, if both parties were US citizens, all taxes would be deferred until the second spouse passed away. This situation need not create unreasonable hardship for the non-citizen as long as the couple complies with the rule concerning co-trusteeship.

Unfortunately, experience since the passing of the legislation demonstrates that very few individuals are aware of the problem. Consequently, little has been done by those who are known to be residents and not citizens to correct their estate planning to provide for the solution granted by Congress through co-trusteeship or sole trusteeship of a US citizen or trust institution.

Careful drafting is necessary. This again demonstrates the critical need for qualified tax counsel and advice from financial planners and accountants to ensure that this trap does not put an undue burden on the family members, regardless of their citizenship.

In situations where there is dual citizenship, a co-trusteeship should be used to ensure that the 100 percent marital deduction would be maintained for the benefit of the family.

9

Some Problems as Estates Grow Larger

Introduction

The title of this chapter has been very carefully chosen. The reason for this is that estates usually continue to grow larger from the time they are first examined by an attorney.

Unfortunately, there is, in fact, a perception within the public that their particular estate does not grow as rapidly as they normally do.

With nearly fifty years of experience in either the insurance world or the legal world, I have consistently noted that estates as a general proposition double every ten years.

I have tested this hypothesis on a practical basis with innumerable clients. They always seem surprised when I ask them to start with the age they are now, go back ten years and look at the size of their estates; and then go back another ten years and so forth and look at the size of their estates. It is a rare exception where the estate has not grown significantly.

One specific example may be particularly helpful.

In early spring, three years ago, a discussion was held at some length concerning this issue with a couple who had emigrated from China approximately thirty years ago. In looking back over his life, he had come to the conclusion that he had probably reached his peak in terms of ability to earn money.

As stated, this discussion took place in the spring of 2011. A subsequent meeting took place in November 2011 to provide for a more clear analysis. He, his wife, and his accountant came and visited me concerning the potential tax problems that they may face three years from now, assuming there are no further changes in the tax laws.

We projected it out to 2014. The accountant was convinced that by that year, this date, the estate would double again, as had been the history of the estate for many years. This is a classic example where it would be very helpful to have serious talks with, not only clients, but also their other advisors.

It is unusual that the estate would double every three years, but that has been a consistent pattern for a significant number of years.

Haun was an interesting individual. He described having arrived in San Francisco at age nineteen and deciding that he was going to be an American in every sense of the word of adopting the culture, learning the language, and working diligently for the benefit of his family. He succeeded in every respect from a financial standpoint as well as family history. His three children are now college educated and are becoming well established. He owns a successful business with more than fifty employees. The likelihood of its growth doubling by the year 2006 was probably conservative.

Haun recalled how intently I had looked the couple in the eye early in the year when they wanted to dispute the suggestion I made that estates commonly double every ten years. I had suggested to them that when people like them worked hard, were bright, and worked with integrity to provide a quality product or service, it was difficult to fail in the American economy. They now believe that.

With that type of introduction, it is important to understand that the story of Haun and his good wife is not unusual. My experiences demonstrated that even though people do not necessarily become unusually wealthy as these two have become, they often become comfortable, and as they grow older, contrary to their perception, their estates do not diminish in size. They normally continue to grow.

The Nature of Estate Planning

There is a sense of irony when someone comes to an attorney requesting assistance to do estate planning and after quality work has been completed, they assume that no further work will need to be done. This is certainly a misconception. This is like buying a new automobile in the finest condition and of the highest of quality, and believing that after driving it for a hundred thousand miles, a significant amount of work, tune-ups, and a significant amount of care do not need to be utilized.

Or the individual purchasing a new home believing that they no longer will need to have either a different home or that significant repairs were not going to be made on the existing home over a period of time.

If it is important to understands that the nature of estate planning is not an event. The nature of estate planning is that it is a process of ever tuning and re-tuning. It is a process of modifying and utilizing the vehicles available at a particular time as the law changes. It is a process whereby a larger estate will require additional tuning and more vehicles will need to be introduced with ever-increasing care required on behalf of the individual and the family to ensure that what they have in place by way of estate planning will serve their ultimate goals.

Therefore, it is imperative that the attorney, financial planner, etc., understand the important part on a very personal level, that they play an important part in the lives of their clients.

In contrast to most areas of the law, which are adversarial in nature, it is hoped that the estate planning process can remain one that is not adversarial per se. Although this cannot always be true, it should be the primary goal. Unfortunately, that hope is contrary to what is perceived to be happening more constantly in the legal world.

For example:

> In one state, if a family member files a petition for conservatorship by virtue of a seriously and perhaps fatally disabled parent, the court, as a matter of law, must appoint an attorney to represent that individual to make sure that the integrity of the adversarial system is maintained.

By the way, where possible, the petitioner, or the family, or the individual who is the conservator, must pay the cost of both attorneys. In that particular state, under examination, the court is also required to appoint an independent investigator. By the time the process is done, it is difficult to spend less than $5,000 to $10,000 just for the first year.

The estate planner is in a unique position in that they can help circumvent the insanity of the direction of the legal system in believing that things can only be settled in a courtroom in an adversarial setting. The profession itself seems to continue to promote the belief in the validity of that approach in suggesting that, if there is a better one, show it to them. When I hear that statement, the only thing I can assume is that the individual has never looked at other systems throughout the Western world.

I had significant interface with the British system and the Canadian system. You can be assured that the kinds of insanity of the insistence of an adversarial system under any and all legal relationships is looked upon with the appropriate disdain as it is developing in the United States.

What is being suggested is the necessity of adjustments and introductions of new systems and possibilities that will add to the capacity of the family to maintain control of the estate, minimize administrative costs, and save significant taxes during life and at the time of death, even on small- and medium-sized estates. One last event may be helpful to make this point to the reader. Earlier in my career, I had the opportunity of meeting Norman Dacey. As you may know, Norman Dacey wrote the book titled, *How to Avoid Probate* in about 1965.

In discussing his book with him, I said that he seemed to start from four premises, which were:

1. Everyone should avoid probate.
2. The avoidance of probate could probably be best accomplished through the use of a trust.
3. Everyone should minimize his or her death taxes.
4. All attorneys were dishonest.

He smiled and said that I had correctly understood his text.

I told him that I was sure that he was correct on the first three items, but I was not sure about the fourth. I then explained to him that I had a partner who I knew was honest. He laughed and told me he understood the point.

My experiences with those who are deeply involved in the estate planning process are generally sincere, competent attorneys. Those who have carried that on into the elder law area of estate planning have demonstrated themselves to be caring individuals who often give extraordinary amounts of time, efforts, and emotional energy with little return in the practice of the profession.

The One Important Constant in our Lives

It has been consistently said that the only two certain things in life are death and taxes.

Indeed, it is agreed that death is inevitable. However, as tax exemptions increase and individuals allow themselves to become more sophisticated in the estate planning process, the possibility of avoiding death taxes is very real. It is suggested that by the year 2012, with careful planning, no more than 2 percent of the people in the United States should be paying any death taxes. However, that will not happen because people are intransigent in their willingness to learn new techniques and expend a small amount of money on the most important business that they will ever have during their life. That is their own personal financial affairs. They will spend untold amounts of time and money in their business, trade, or profession to make it a success, but seem to be unwilling to spend a relatively small amount of money to make sure that the business of their family wealth is properly structured and managed.

Although it would appear that death and taxes are certainties, there is another element that should always be kept in mind, and that is the likelihood of change. Anything that an estate planner tells you today may not be true next year. Any document that an attorney prepares for you regarding a living will declaration or power of attorney for health care, no matter how well drafted, may have to be changed four years from now because the legislatures in every state insist on continually tinkering and changing the written requirements.

There has been no attempt to justify what the legislature or Congress does in continually making changes. It is just a fact of life that the only real constant that you need to be concerned about is the reality of change. Change is immutable.

In the remaining portion of this chapter, a fairly cursory examination will be made of two areas that are particularly usable in larger estates that need to be addressed. However, in this examination it will be readily seen that the very problem of change is the fundamental problem.

Generation Skipping Transfer Tax

Suggesting that there are too many writings concerning the generation skipping exemption is an understatement. The very title is misleading. In reading it, one may believe that there is some type of exemption that can be utilized by the use of some form of generation skipping trust or some other type of vehicle that gives a useful exemption.

In fact, the generation skipping tax per se is intended to limit the ability of any family to pass wealth on past each generation without having it taxed by the federal government. There seems to be a preconceived idea that the US government has a better capacity to manage wealth for the benefit of the public than the businessperson who has developed a business where many people are hired. As a general proposition, most of us understand that the taxation of an estate at the time of death is the most hideous form of double taxation imposed by the US government.

However, the so-called "exclusion" provides a method in larger estates where money can be set aside, up to $2 million, by a husband and wife in a trust system, whereby the $2 million may be utilized in a form of a life estate for the benefit of children and then passed on to the grandchildren without being taxed again under the Federal Estate Death Tax system. Instead of an exemption, this whole matter of the generation skipping transfer tax should be perceived as a punitive tax.

Similarly, if a couple desires to make gifts either during life or upon death, they are able to gift in a form that will allow for the skipping of one generation of taxation, provided the gift does not exceed the $2 million limit.

However, the history of the legislation in 1976 is very instructive.

The primary legislation with all its great confusion came into existence in 1976. At that time, it was not clear that anybody could develop a trust system, either on a testamentary basis or on a living trust basis that could escape the punitive tax that is imposed for attempting to skip a generation of taxes.

The Treasury Regulations and Revenue Rulings and case law became so convoluted that several attempts were made during the 80s to make the system workable so that there could be some certainty in the method by which estate planning could exist where some generation skipping could be accomplished.

Finally, in the early 1990s, Congress passed legislation that makes it fairly clear that a transfer of $2 million or $1 million per person can be made in a way that it will be taxed upon their death, but not taxed again on the death of their children. Hence, when the funds reach the grandchildren, there will indeed be a skipping of death taxes between their children and their grandchildren, up to the maximum amount allowed.

This area of the law is extremely complex. Only those attorneys who have serious time and effort have any business attempting to draft documents of this character. Fortunately, high-quality material is available for attorneys who are willing to spend the time. Probably the most articulate analysis that has been prepared is by Professor Jerry Kasner in his two-volume text, *Post Mortem Tax Planning*. It has grown substantially each year, and in all probability that growth will continue. The entire text is obviously not dedicated to generation skipping transfer taxes. But a substantial portion of it is either directly or indirectly related to the subject.

Therefore, if one desires to minimize the taxes on the family wealth, then the subject of generation skipping transfer tax and exclusions need to be discussed at some length with an attorney and/or accountant or financial advisors. Eventually, an attorney must be engaged to do proper drafting.

To help you understand, a simple example is shown in Illustration 9-1. It would be possible upon the death of both spouses to transfer $2 million to a generation skipping transfer trust, which would provide that all income must be distributed to the children beneficiaries. Upon their demise, the assets would then be transferred to their children, either equally or some other form acceptable to the initiators of the estate plan.

Illustration 9-1

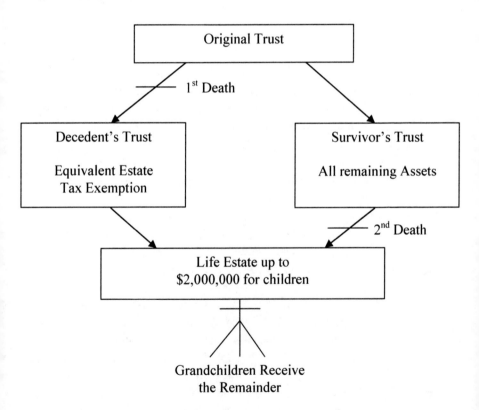

In making this statement and using this diagram, a certain fear is inherent in even discussing it, in such short form. Criticism may be raised that it is an oversimplification and in a sense, that is true. However, it is felt that an oversimplification as a beginning place is better than no discussion at all.

Charitable Lead Trust

There has been much public discussion by many universities, hospitals, and other types of charitable entities in the use of the charitable remainder trusts. However, there is a minimal amount of writing for the public on the subject of the charitable lead trust.

It is suggested, however, that in many instances the charitable lead trust is a far more efficient vehicle for family wealth preservation than is the charitable remainder trust.

In simple terms, a charitable remainder trust is an arrangement whereby wealth in some form is transferred to a trust with the donors retaining a life income of not less than 5 percent annually of the amount gifted. At the time of the death of the donor, or the donors, then the remaining principal amount is delivered free of tax to the charity. This has the advantage of taking that particular gift into trust out of the taxable estate and provides some income tax benefits in the interim. To make it easier to visualize this kind of arrangement, an examination of Illustration 9-2 may be helpful.

Illustration 9-2 Charitable Remainder Trust

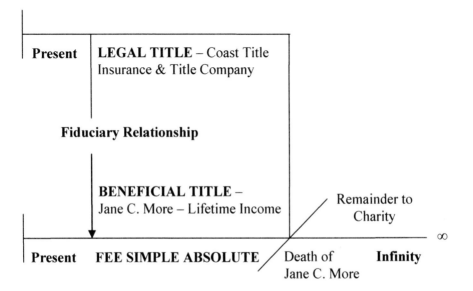

The total asset is treated as fee simple absolute. However, the timeline from the time the trust is established through infinity is broken into two portions. The first is a retained life estate based on either a dollar amount or a percentage of the trust that is to go on an annual basis to the donors. At the death of the donors, the estate is then transferred into fee simple absolute free of trust to the charity. The charitable lead trust works in the reverse.

The charitable lead trust, as demonstrated in Illustration 9-3, is one in which for a term of years, all income from the trust is paid to a charitable institution.

Illustration 9-3 Charitable Lead Trust

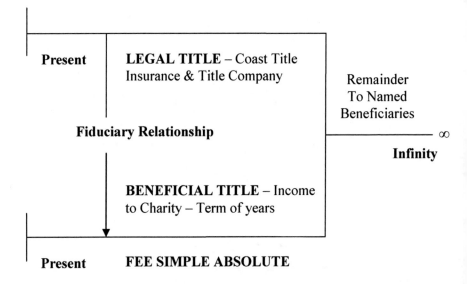

This is based on a fairly complex formula through the rules and regulations that have been issued through the Treasury Department in what are known as Treasury Regulations and in various Revenue Rulings that are publicized by the Internal Revenue Service. As long as one follows the rules and plays the game and uses reasonable conservative estimates, an independent trustee, and a valid donative intent to a legitimate charity, then after the terms of years, which will normally be from thirteen to seventeen, the remaining assets of the principle of the trust will revert to the named beneficiaries of those who have established the trust. For example, if a couple has a substantially large estate and they desire that a portion of it be deferred in its delivery to their children, then they can transfer it to a trust leaving the flow of income, in accordance with the appropriate formula, to a favorite charitable institution such as a university, church, or medical research organization such as a cancer society. Then, after the term of years, the remaining asset will revert to their children or whomever they name.

If they have left a substantial net estate to the children, then the children will have the benefit of having the use of those funds during the period of the charitable lead trust. Then the beneficiaries receive an infusion of more funds that will not be taxed for death tax purposes by virtue of the very nature of the charitable lead trust. The substance of the charitable lead trust is that Congress has allowed an individual to have assets withheld from being taxed in an estate if the income is paid to a charitable institution for a sufficient period of time. Functionally, this is the reverse of the charitable remainder trust with the charitable entity receiving the benefits at the beginning of the establishment of the trust instead of upon the death of the donors. Obviously, this is a very complicated arrangement.

Nonetheless, this vehicle is a very viable approach for maintaining the wealth for the family through allowable avoidance of death taxes through an interim gift of income to a charity.

Conclusion

Two examples have been used for two sophisticated arrangements whereby death taxes can be minimized. Many others could be cited. By way of example, in Chapter 14 there is a fairly thorough analysis of how a use of a charitable remainder trust joined with the use of life insurance to maintain the integrity of the estate for a family

However, it is hoped that, through these illustrations, the reader will understand and be guided to do analysis with competent advisors as to how they can maintain control of their estate as long as possible, how administrative costs can be minimized, and how various kinds of taxes can be either minimized or eliminated.

10

The Non-Traditional Family

Introduction

This chapter is intended to cover situations such as the following:

1. Two individuals of the same sex living together as a family unit;
2. Two individuals of opposite sexes living together as a family unit without the benefit of matrimony; or
3. Siblings residing together as a family unit, sharing expenses and earnings.

In any of these situations, it is possible to have all but one of the benefits of the traditional family in the estate-planning process, provided all documents are properly drawn and that ownership of property is shared on an equal basis.

Strategies

If we examine Illustration 10-1 with Illustration 10-2, we see that by changing names it is possible to preserve the $1 million tax exemption in 2001 for each individual. This amount will increase to $2 million per individual through a phase-in by 2006 and $5 million per person in years 2011 and 2012. Changing names will also make it possible to have all of the other benefits of a trust. These benefits include: limitation of probate upon the death of both parties; maximum privacy; maximum control by trustors; distribution of assets to the beneficiaries in the way that is desired; and the care of either or both individuals in the event of serious or total disability.

Illustration 10-1

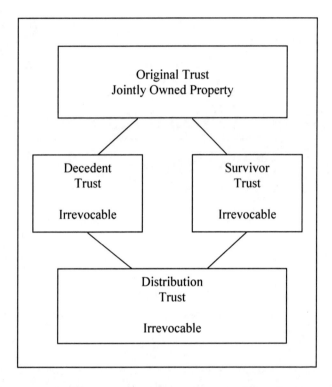

Individuals who acquire property may treat the relationship and earnings as a partnership arrangement between them. However, it is recommended that there be a clear acknowledgment of the relationship. The only way to make that type of clear acknowledgment is through a formal declaration of property ownership rights.

A simple declaration that the parties are treating all properties as owned as tenants in common, with each party owning an undivided 50-percent interest, should be sufficient. This recommendation is the same for any non-traditional family either in a common law state or a community property state. If such a declaration might create a present gifting problem, it should be reviewed with your advisors. Some states allow for a formal contract.

A non-traditional family can save future taxation on an estate, in the same way that a traditional family can. The decedent's trust can provide for the increase in value of the principal within the decedent's trust. As previously indicated, if one party dies, and half of the estate is attributable to the decedent's trust, and that trust is irrevocable. The assets attributed to that trust could be held as a life estate with reasonably principal invasion rights for the survivor party.

When the second person dies, the property in the decedent trust representing the first of the two to die, will not be subjected to death taxes, since it would have already been taxed. Consequently, any equity growth would pass on in the same manner, as would be the case with a traditional family. Therefore, the only amount that would be taxed is that which exceeded the equivalent estate tax exemption in force in the year of death under the survivor's trust.

The survivor can minimize taxation on the second death even though the estate of the survivor may well have grown substantially each year. To minimize taxes, the survivor should use not only income, but also principal from the survivor's trust before consuming the principal of the decedent's trust.

A Trust versus a Will

It seems particularly advantageous for those who have a relationship that may be considered non-traditional to use this type of arrangement, not only to avoid probate and minimize taxes, but also to maintain a maximum of privacy concerning their affairs.

Unlike a will, it is very difficult to attack the credibility and legal status of a trust. The reason for this is easy to understand. The competency level required to sign a will is simply to be able to "recognize the natural object of affection." This is such a low requirement that it opens a will to attack on the basis of duress, undue influence, fraud, and a multitude of other grounds. An attack might well be based on an argument of one person's capacity to have excessive influence in either legitimate or nefarious ways upon a partner with whom he or she resides.

For example, if the will was not drawn until there was a serious illness, the will is even more subject to attack. Often such an attack leads to a substantial financial loss to the estate because of the litigation process. It also publicizes matters that both parties may prefer to keep private.

On the other hand, the complexity of the estate planning process using a trust requires a fairly astute analysis. The client must demonstrate a high capacity of understanding of what he or she is trying to accomplish. As a consequence, trusts are very seldom successfully attacked. The level of competency to use a trust suggests the need to be able to contract.

It is recommended that the following six steps be taken in the order given.

Recommended Procedures

1. The parties must be sure their relationship is a viable one, which they want to treat as permanent.
2. The parties should make a simple declaration acknowledging that their properties are being commingled from that time forward, taking care that there is not an inadvertent gift, where a contribution by one party exceeds that of the other party. This can cause the imposition of gift taxes, either federal and/or state.
3. It may be necessary for some assets owned by one person to be maintained separately for a number of years. However, there can be ongoing transfers through gifting under the exclusion rules by one party to the other. Ultimately, all of the assets are transferred without any gift tax being imposed. If the parties are willing to use their gift tax exemption during life through life gifting, in most cases their estates will eventually be readjusted to the point where all property is owned as tenants in common, with each party owning an undivided one-half interest.
4. Counsel familiar with this process and unbiased about the parties' living arrangements should be engaged. Each party should consider using separate counsel for clarification of the legal implications of what is being accomplished, especially where one or both estates are large at the time the arrangement is contemplated.
5. Counsel should then draft documents allowing the parties to share their interests in a manner similar to that shown in Illustration 10-2,

with all the characteristics of the family program shown in Illustration 10-1.

6. The parties would then sign the documents and implement the arrangement by transferring existing assets into the trust and then continue the administration of the assets as belonging to the new legal entity.

Benefit Unavailable to a Non-Traditional Family

The only benefit unavailable to the non-traditional family arrangement is the establishment of a trust or any other vehicle to provide for deferral of taxation under the 100 percent marital deduction. For example, a $4 million estate is owned based on an undivided one-half interest held by each party. When one of the couple dies, his or her half of the estate ($2 million) would be subject to taxation.

I have participated in the preparation and implementation of many arrangements of this type and assisted with settlement of the estates when a death occurred. It has proven to be a very workable arrangement for people who fall into the non-traditional family category.

11

Using the Irrevocable Trust

Introduction

The primary use of a revocable trust is to plan for federal estate taxes and ensure the efficient and effective transfer of assets at the death of an individual or a couple. In comparison, the primary uses of an irrevocable trust are to minimize income taxes, to transfer property to individuals during their lifetime in a way that is cost- and tax-efficient, and to maximize protection against creditors.

Making Gifts to Minors

Methods by which individuals can make gifts to minors are established under state law or accomplished under an alternate use of federal law. The state laws are normally versions of what is known as the Uniform Gifts to Minors Act (UGMA). Under this legislation, a person is designated as a custodian through whom the parents or others can make gifts to minors under the law of their state of residence. The age of majority for this purpose will vary from state to state—from under eighteen to twenty-one. Under this arrangement, the gift is made to the custodian for the benefit of the minor and is required to be distributed to the minor when he or she reaches the state's age of majority, which is often age eighteen.

The federal approach is included in Internal Revenue Code section 2503(c).[8] Under §2503(c) there are basically two approaches that can be

---

[8] I.R.C. §2503(c) (1998).

used. The first allows a husband and wife or any other person to establish an irrevocable trust naming a non-controlled person as the trustee and the minor as the beneficiary. For example, if parents decide to make gifts to a minor child to establish a college fund, a formal trust document would be drawn, naming a trustee to manage those funds until the beneficiary reaches twenty-one. At that time, the statute requires that distribution be made outright. Regardless of the age at which gifts are made to a minor, until the child reaches age fourteen, the income is taxed at the same rate as the child's parents. This same taxation problem applies not only to trusts under the federal legislation, but also under the Uniform Gifts to Minors Act.

In the interim, funds from the trust can be used by the trustee to assist a child in his or her college education or other financial needs. However, great care must be taken to ensure that the trustee does not pay costs that are the legal obligation of the parents, such as providing for the basic necessities of life for the minor child. If that happens, the income tax exemption that the parents enjoy for that child may be forfeited.

This is similar to the Uniform Gifts to Minors Act, except that the trustee, in the federal scheme, often has broader powers beyond simply determining what investments may be held within the portfolio. In many states, UGMA distribution must take place at the age of eighteen under any and all circumstances, as compared to age twenty-one under the federal legislation. The child may be better served by having the funds held irrevocably until age twenty-one. Those three years are often the difference between making the distribution to a child and making the distribution to a reasonably mature adult.

The second approach under the federal legislation allows for gifts in trust to be made to an individual under an arrangement where the trustee is required to make distributions of income on an annual basis or more frequently. When the child reaches a stated age in the trust, which may be at the discretion of those who bring the trust into existence, the principal is distributed. This is also an irrevocable trust. During the period of the trust, the principal is totally protected from creditors of the ultimate beneficiary.

If there is a desire to make gifts to a minor with the trust corpus not distributed until he or she is much older than twenty-one, Illustration 11-1 shows how the funds can be distributed to an Internal Revenue Code §2503(b) trust with mandatory distribution at age forty-five (or any age the trustors feel is appropriate). In the interim, all income is distributed to a §2503(c) trust. The accumulated income will be distributed to the child at twenty-one years of age.

If the §2503(b) trust is used, the gift cannot be made directly to the trustee. If made directly to the beneficiary, who in turn transfers the funds to the trustee, there is no problem. The problem can also be circumvented with what is known as a "Crummey provision." This writer will leave that for your attorney to explain.

Illustration 11-1 IRC §2503(c) Trust

Original Trust

Trustors:	Thomas O. More and Jane C. More
Trustees:	Harold B. Baldridge
Property:	Real and Personal
Powers:	As specified in Trust document
Amendable:	Not in any way
Irrevocable:	Totally
Beneficiary:	Eric N. More, or as specified by beneficiary in the event of his death, or by laws of intestate succession

Eric N. More reaches age 21, then complete distribution of all accumulated income and all principal takes place

Federal legislation that controls how IRC 2503 trusts are managed and taxed has been in existence for more than fifty years; hence a long enough period for maturing by court interpretation for anyone to have confidence in the approach.

The Clifford Trust

Since the Tax Reform Act of 1986, many practitioners believe that the Clifford Trust, or a Ten Years Plus One Day Trust, has been eliminated as a meaningful planning vehicle. For purposes of transferring taxation to another person, this is certainly true. However, the Clifford Trust remains a very useful technique for transferring assets for the benefit of another individual in a vehicle that protects the asset from creditors. This creditor protection continues throughout the term of the trust, even though the tax benefit of using the lower tax rates of the child or other beneficiaries as compared to his or her parents is no longer available.

For example, if a child desires to support an elderly parent and wants to be sure the funds are not subject to claims from creditors, using a Clifford Trust with a term of not less than ten years and one day, ensures that the income will flow safely to the parent. At the end of the term of the irrevocable trust, the primary asset will be transferred back to the grantor or to a named beneficiary(s).

As another example, if a husband and wife desire to provide support for one or more of their parents, and they own a ten-unit apartment complex, they can transfer ownership of the complex into an irrevocable trust for ten years and one day. The apartment house is then available for funding the parents' needs by virtue of the fact that the trust would direct that all income generated by the assets held in the irrevocable trust is to be distributed to the parents. During this time, the benefit of asset protection would be maintained. During the existence of this kind of irrevocable trust, income will be taxed at the children's rates (or the grantor's rate); therefore, there is no income tax savings as was the case before the 1986 Tax Act.

An Irrevocable Trust as a Beneficiary of Life Insurance

An irrevocable trust that is a beneficiary of life insurance, or the owner of life insurance, may have significant value for those persons whose property may be subject to creditor attack either during their lifetimes or upon death.

For example, suppose a physician's wife establishes an irrevocable trust, either with a minimal amount of funds such as $100, or with no funds. If her state law allows such a trust, it would be possible for that trust to continue to exist until the death of her husband.

If, immediately after establishing this trust, the non-professional wife acts as applicant, owner, and premium payor on a life insurance policy on her husband, upon the doctor's death, the funds can be designated to flow into the irrevocable trust. This ensures that the wife and heirs are protected against the doctor's creditors as far as the insurance proceeds that would flow to the trust.

A more specific example demonstrates a way to ensure that insurance funds will not be subject to death taxation by either the state or federal government and to ensure the funds will be available to the surviving family without being subjected to creditors' attacks for any type of claim that may be made against the estate of the deceased professional.

Irrevocable Trust as a Contingent Owner of Life Insurance

In using the credit-bypass trust discussed in Chapter 4, it may also be appropriate to establish an irrevocable trust with the sole purpose of serving as contingent owner of a life insurance policy on the life of one or both of the spouses. Illustration 11-2 demonstrates such an arrangement. However, in certain cases, it can be of substantial economic value to a family in avoiding death taxes when the insured dies. It is unfortunate that few estate planning professionals understand that there are complex issues surrounding the methods of handling a contingent owner of a policy of life insurance. One wonders if most even know that it exists.

Illustration 11-2

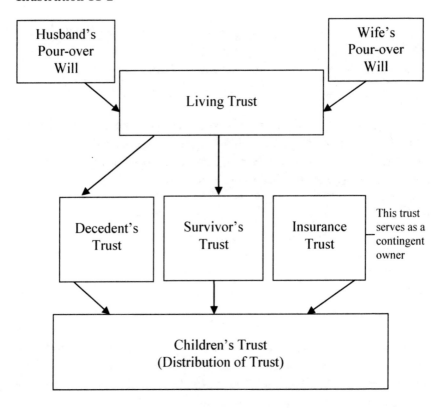

A wife may act as applicant, owner, premium payor, and primary beneficiary of a life insurance policy on her husband. If all funds are paid out of her sole and separate property, and she dies before her husband, ownership of the policy would flow to her husband through the laws of intestacy to become part of his estate at his death.

If, however, the contingent owner is named as the insurance trust shown in Illustration 11-2, then the policy will immediately become owned by the irrevocable trust upon the wife's death. As long as the husband cannot have control over the insurance policy, which would grant him "incidents of ownership," then the insurance policy proceeds can pass to the children at the husband's death without the burden of death taxes on either the state or federal level.

If, after the wife dies, and the insurance policy has as its contingent owner, the insurance trust, as shown in Illustration 11-2, additional premiums, if needed, can either be paid from the cash value of the policy, or by gifts made to the trust by the ultimate beneficiaries or even by the insured, provided these gifts do not exceed the annual exclusion limits. The type of trust is one where counsel will recommend what is known as a "Crummey Provision." This should be discussed with an attorney *before* an insurance application is signed.

Charitable Remainder Trusts

This type of irrevocable trust allows an individual to make a gift to a charity and have an interest in property, which will leave the individual with a lifetime income interest within the parameters allowed by law. Upon death, the assets that remain become solely owned by the charity. This has the advantage of taking the asset out of the estate for federal and state death tax purposes and can provide a substantial income tax benefit through the deductions allowed during lifetime for making gifts to charities.

For instance, if a person makes a gift of $100,000 to a qualified charitable institution, then that institution may be able to pay the grantor 7 or 8 percent of the amount each year as a guaranteed annuity. Upon the death of the grantor, the asset belongs to the charity and is not included in the decedent's estate. In the interim, a formula is used that is published in the Internal Revenue Code and Treasury Regulations to determine an amount of credit against the income taxes of the individual making the gift.

The charitable remainder trust is a highly sophisticated type of planning and one that should be undertaken only with careful consideration and the best possible advice of competent counsel.

Sometimes those who promote charitable remainder trusts seem to forget the fundamental law that there must be intent to make a gift to a particular charity and that the gift must not be merely for purposes of tax avoidance. For example, if a person is persuaded to make a gift to an organization of which the person has no knowledge, either directly or indirectly, and the person merely wants to avoid taxation, then there is a high possibility that the gift will be rejected by the Internal Revenue Service because there was no charitable donative intent.

Special Needs Trust and Medicaid Trusts

As people age and/or encounter disability, they face the problem of getting and retaining access to state and federal assistance such as Medicare and Social Security or some form of state aid. Often individuals are first required to dissipate the assets they have acquired during their lifetimes. One of the methods of ensuring that an individual is able to maintain access to federal and state benefits is the use of a relatively new type of trust vehicles, commonly known as a special needs trust or a Medicaid trust.

Because of the relative novelty of these trusts, the draftsman should properly disclose uncertainty as to the viability of such an arrangement. The government seems to be somewhat fickle about requirements, rules, and regulations that may be imposed at any given time. The general approach of the government agencies is that when such a change is made, the government simply takes the position that the new set of rules has always been the law.

This is not to suggest that these trusts should not be used. It has problems, but they are probably the best vehicle in current existence for maximizing a family's capacity to maintain the integrity of the family's wealth and still receive benefits from federal and state agencies to which the family has contributed over a significant number of years.

For example, if a family has a child who has a serious disability, such as Down Syndrome, it would be possible for a certain portion within their family trust to be allocated to be poured into a special needs trust for the benefit of the disabled child at the time the parents die. The trust provisions would specify that no benefits would be made available to the child in the place of benefits that would be available through government agencies if the trust did not exist.

This subject will continue to be an area of controversy, and the usefulness of these trusts will require ongoing monitoring. This is particularly true since Congress has passed legislation that may make it a criminal offense for an attorney to either advise the use of such trusts or assist in drafting and implementation of them. Fortunately, the legislation was declared unconstitutional by the US Supreme Court. Nonetheless, the "god of Washington" will continue to attempt to minimize the use of either the special needs trust or a Medicaid trust.

12

Working with Attorneys and Other Professionals

Introduction

Financial planners and insurance underwriters seem to have more difficulty than other professionals do in attempting to work with the legal and accounting professions. There are some notable exceptions to this, but there appear to be some deep-seated antagonisms, which go back many years and create great difficulties when these professionals attempt to work together. This is a serious issue because much estate planning is accomplished through the good offices of the insurance underwriter or the financial planner.

For attorneys, this antagonism has its roots, to some extent, in law school. In law school texts, many of the cases involved revolve around situations where insurance companies, particularly in the casualty area, have gone to extremes to take advantage of the public.

The entire concept of cases based on "bad faith" and "unfair dealings" comes from one of the cases referred to above. One case resulted in $5 million in punitive damages awarded on a relatively small claim involving inappropriate conduct by the insurance company. After three years of studying case after case of this kind, it is not surprising that the law school student develops a low opinion of the insurance industry. Unfortunately, there is no distinction made in law school between the methods of operation of casualty insurance companies and those of life insurance companies.

This is not to suggest that there are no problems within life insurance companies, but generally, the vast majority of the serious, unpleasant problems have developed from cases involving non-life insurance products. It is fair to say that if an individual has not entered into an insurance contract with a life insurer fraudulently, and has given truthful information in the application, then upon death, the policy pays. This is not always the case with casualty insurance. That is because there is a secondary industry involved with the casualty insurance business.

The secondary industry involves adjusters. Their primary responsibility is to meet with the injured party, whether the injury is to themselves or their property, in an attempt to settle the matter at the lowest possible cost to the insurance company. Often the adjusters' own compensation consists either totally or is a percentage of the amount of reduction they can negotiate in payment of the claim. This can create an unsavory situation, and serious antagonisms have resulted.

The financial planner and the life underwriter should take the time to become acquainted with counsel representing their clients and work as closely as possible in a team approach to bring about quality estate planning, which takes into account all relevant issues. The primary issue for all is usually the funding mechanism for supporting the family or beneficiaries when the death of the breadwinner occurs and for payment of death taxes upon the demise of both parents. These are often accomplished with life insurance products without the unsavory problems extended in the casualty business.

Strategies

One technique is to find financial planners or life insurance underwriters who have been prominent in a particular geographic area for an extended period of time. Senior bank officers, who have been with their institution for many years, are another good choice. Usually, these professionals are thoroughly familiar with members of the legal profession and are sensitive to all of the issues involved in estate planning. They are also usually willing to work with other professionals for the ultimate benefit of the public.

You can access names of attorneys through the state bar associations. Unfortunately, in many cases, incompetent attorneys are located through referrals, and the service is no better than if you picked an attorney from an advertisement in the Yellow Pages.

Finally, readers should regard with caution the seminar programs being presented to the public throughout the United States. Seminars can be useful and worthwhile, but it is important to exercise caution regarding which programs you choose. If the program is sponsored by people who are highly qualified in the area and who have demonstrated over time that they can be trusted, it may be useful to attend the seminar. However, even where sponsors are competent in estate planning, it is not unusual for a so-called free planning seminar to be nothing more than a prospecting technique for salespersons. Often there is little concern for the public. The primary aim is a commission at all costs.

There are also law firms that do wholesale estate planning through trusts by pre-programming the vast majority of trusts, with little concern for the details that are so critical in providing quality estate plans that reflect the desires and needs of a particular family. Any time someone offers a substantial bargain in this area, the buyer should beware.

Finally, there are books in the marketplace written by those who, if their own lives were examined, would demonstrate no competency in telling others how to organize their lives. No matter how compelling and authoritative the text may appear, it is vital to look to competent individuals within the legal profession and quality financial planners who have both the expertise and time to provide sound advice. Estate planning is highly complex. Those who have not acquired proper credentials should be suspect. If the financial advisor has a CFP, CHFP, or CLU, then they should have a willingness to at least go through reasonable education.

However, non-attorneys who have the temerity to draft trusts should be shunned.

13

Compilation of Estate Information and Trust Implementation

Introduction - Use of a Simple Questionnaire

Often, the amount of information the estate planner (attorney, financial planner, or life insurance agent) requests of the client is overwhelming. A fairly simple method of compiling sufficient information for the planner is outlined in Illustration 13-1.

Date Prepared_____

ESTATE PLANNING QUESTIONNAIRE

FULL NAME _____ **Date of Birth** _____
Other Names _____

Check One: Married ☐   Single ☐   Divorced ☐   Widowed ☐

SPOUSE'S FULL NAME _____ **Date of Birth** _____
Other Names _____

ADDRESS_____
    City _____   County _____
    State _____   Zip Code _____

PHONE NUMBERS: Residence   (____) _____
                      Fax   (____) _____

Man's Work   (____) _____
Woman's Work (____) _____
Email Address   _____

U.S. Citizen: Man Yes □ No □   **Woman** Yes □ No □

If no, Citizen of what Country?   If no, Citizen of what Country?

_____   _____

Social Security Number of Husband _____
Social Security Number of Wife _____

CHILDREN

FULL NAMES (Please print)	LIVING		DATE OF BIRTH OR AGE	MARRIED		NUMBER OF CHILDREN (Your Grandchildren, if any)
	Yes	No		Yes	No	

A.   REAL PROPERTY   Method of Holding Real Property

*Please use following designations as to the Method of Holding listed below -- **J/T** - Joint Tenancy; **T/E** - Tenancy by the Entirety; **T/C** Tenancy in Common; **S/O** - Single Owner; or **C/P** - Community Property:

Address	Estimated Fair Market Value	Method of Holding*	Amount of Outstanding Indebtedness

AT THE TIME THAT YOU COME TO REVIEW DRAFTS, PLEASE ALSO BRING PHOTOCOPIES OF ALL DEEDS TO REAL PROPERTY AND THEIR RELATED REAL PROPERTY TAX BILLS.

Any explanation needed as to nature of property or ownership rights: (E.g., subject to Pre or Post Nuptial Agreement)

List all foreign owned property of any kind:

Income from all sources (average for past two (2) years) $_____

B.   PERSONAL PROPERTY

Please use following designations as to how listed items are held --
J/T - Joint Tenancy; T/E - Tenancy by the Entirety; T/C Tenancy in
Common; S/O - Single Owner; or C/P - Community Property:

1.   **Total in Savings Accounts** $_____ Held in _____

2.   **Total in Bonds** $_____ Held in _____

3.   **Total Stock Value** $_____ Held in _____

4.   **Jewelry Value** $_____

5.   **Safety Deposit Box(es)**   Yes □   No □
                                      Location:

_____

_____

_____

6.   **Describe any interest owned in Pension Plans, IRA's, Tax
      Deferred Annuities.**

      Husband   **Wife**

7.   List any other real property, personal property and location.

8.   Insurance Policies:

	Policy #1	Policy #2	Policy #3
Insured:			
Insurance Company:			
Face Amount:			
Term Life or Whole Life:			
Beneficiary:			
Policy Owner:			
Policy Applicant:			
Premium Payor:			

If there are additional policies, please describe below.

_____

_____

_____

_____

_____

_____

ESTATE PLANNING QUESTIONNAIRE CHECKLIST

Do not complete information on this page, this is a summary only. Space to complete this information is on following pages. If more space is needed add additional pages.

A. TRUSTEES

    1. Original
    2. Alternates

B. GUARDIANS OF MINOR CHILDREN (if any)

    1. First
    2. Alternate

C. IMMEDIATE DISTRIBUTION ON DEATH OF EITHER TRUSTOR (if any)

D. DISTRIBUTION ON DEATH OF SURVIVOR (LAST TO DIE)

    1. Immediate, if any
    2. Time of Division, e.g., immediate or at what specific ages
    3. Terms of Division

        a. To Whom?
        b. Amount (dollar or percent)
        c. When?

E. TIME AND MANNER OF DISTRIBUTION

F. CONTINGENT BENEFICIARIES - TERMINATION WITH NO ISSUE SURVIVING

    1. To Whom (e.g., life estate to parents, or split in two halves with one-half for each of the original Trustors' family, etc.)
    2. Time of Distribution

G. SPECIAL INSTRUCTIONS (if any)

H. PERSON(S) TO ACT UNDER DURABLE POWER OF
    ATTORNEY FOR HEALTH CARE

I. LIVING WILL DECLARATION (if any)

J. BURIAL OR CREMATION INSTRUCTIONS

K. ANY GIFTS TO CHARITIES

L. ANY SPECIAL COMMITTEES

**REMEMBER TO COMPLETE THE INFORMATION ON THE
FOLLOWING PAGES**

DETAILED ESTATE PLANNING INFORMATION NEEDED

A. Order of Trustees (Can be one Trustee, or two or more Co-Trustees)

    1. Original

_____

_____

    2. First Alternate

_____

_____

    3. Second Alternate

_____

_____

B. Guardians (if any)

    1. Original

_____

_____

    2. First Alternate (if any)

_____

_____

    3. Second Alternate (if any)

_____

_____

C. Any distribution on Death of First Spouse (if any)

_____

_____

D. Division of Estate Among Beneficiaries on Second Death or upon Death if a single person

_____

_____

_____

E. Time and Manner of Distribution

_____

_____

_____

F. Contingent Beneficiaries (E.g., Parents, Charities, etc.)

_____

_____

_____

G. Special Instructions (E.g., a particular item to a named beneficiary)

_____

_____

_____

H. Person(s) to Act Under Power of Attorney for Health Care

    1. Original _____

        a. Address and Telephone Number

            _____

            _____ (___)_____

   2. First Alternate (if any)_____

        a. Address and Telephone Number

                  _____

                _____ (___)_____

   3. Second Alternate (if any) _____
        a. Address and Telephone Number

                  _____

                _____ (___)_____

I. Living Will Declaration

Yes □   No □

J. Burial or Cremation Instructions

_____
_____

K. Describe any gifts to be made to Charities (if any)

_____
_____

L. Any Special Committees (E.g., Investment Committee or Competency Committee

_____
_____

<u>**ADVISORS**</u>

ACCOUNTANT

Name _____

Address_____

City _____ State _____ Zip Code _____

Telephone Number (___) _____

BROKER(S)

Name _____

Address_____

City _____ State _____ Zip Code _____

Telephone Number (___) _____

LIFE INSURANCE AGENT

Name _____

Address_____

City _____ State _____ Zip Code _____

Telephone Number (___) _____

FINANCIAL PLANNER

Name _____

Address_____

City _____ State _____ Zip Code _____

Telephone Number (___) _____

BANK

Name _____

Address_____

City _____ State _____ Zip Code _____

Telephone Number (___) _____

**USE FOR ANY ADDITIONAL INFORMATION OR
CLARIFICATION**

_____
_____
_____
_____
_____
_____
_____
_____
_____
_____
_____

FEE ARRANGEMENT

_____
_____
_____
_____
_____
_____
_____
_____
_____
_____
_____
_____

This questionnaire has been changed and shortened, as better ways have been found to obtain information. It is not frightening or threatening to the client, yet it provides sufficient information to prepare a beginning draft of estate planning documents. Once this information is gathered, by either a phone call or personal discussion, an initial draft can be produced.

Experience suggests that the best time to get down to serious details would be after the client has reviewed the initial draft. This gives a much clearer understanding of what the estate-planning program accomplishes. It seems almost magical the way words on the written page can bring out people's emotional reactions of "Yes," "This is what I want," or "No, that isn't quite right."

After a second meeting, and a careful review, the draft documents can be revised. This process assures the client that the estate plan being prepared is unique and not part of a preset program, with his or her personal information merely inserted.

Simplicity and personalization are two of the most important aspects of an estate-planning program. Beginning the process with a simple, yet sufficient, questionnaire, which the planner and/or the client can complete at their leisure, greatly reduces the stress involved, and the client does not feel overwhelmed.

Of course, additional and future planning activities by the professional planner may require substantially more information and documentation. When professionals give their assistance a step at a time, the client will quickly gain confidence in their ability to plan and to obtain all of the necessary information.

Transferring Assets to the Trust

Once drafts have been finalized, signed, and properly implemented, the process of transferring assets into the trust should begin. This is normally not the complicated process many planners and clients may believe it to be.

Some transfers, such as real estate to a trust, are made more efficiently by legal counsel. Most assets, however, including stocks, savings, and other accounts, are best handled by the client dealing directly with the institution involved. This allows clients to participate in the process and provides reassurance that their control of the estate has not been taken away.

As implied throughout this guide, the most important aspect of estate planning is the comfort level of the client. The knowledge that control of the estate has not been lost instills confidence that quality estate planning will continue in setting up living trusts.

Financial Institutions

Some financial institutions require a full copy of the trust instrument, but this is not always true. Such demands should be discouraged.

What the institution really wants and requires is evidence that the trust exists and that there is proper authority concerning use of the assets held by the trust. Certification of the trust is the most useful way to accomplish this. Experience has shown that no institution has turned down a certification presented in lieu of a copy of the entire trust instrument. Progressively, financial institutions such as stock brokerage firms have developed their own form of trust certification.

Providing certification is a better choice than giving an institution a copy of the complete trust instrument. Once a full trust document is in the hands of an institution, the possibility of maintaining confidential information will be jeopardized.

Clients must take great care to be sure future assets are acquired in the name of the trust. Counsel must make frequent contacts with the client (either in-person or through correspondence) to be sure this is true. Failure to maintain acquisitions in the name of the trust may result in at least part of the estate being probated. Few situations are more complex and difficult than having some, but not all, of the assets go through the probate process. From a practical standpoint, it may be argued that a client is better served by either funding the trust altogether, or not funding it at all. However, this later will require a probate. Fortunately, it is not difficult for the client to maintain the assets in the name of the trust, so there should be no need to use the pour-over will.

14

Methods of Funding for Death Taxes and Use of Life Insurance

Funding for Death Taxes

In analyzing the methods through which federal estate tax can be funded, the process seems to break down into four fundamental approaches, which are:

1. Funds available through the family's cash flow and existing assets that are readily available by virtue of being in liquid form;
2. Sale of assets to pay death taxes;
3. Borrowing of funds from either a financial institution or the government; and
4. Utilization of some kind of sinking fund, either informally or through some insurance vehicle.

The following is a more detailed analysis of these four approaches from the author's text, Revocable Trusts, under the section life insurance products.

1. *Utilization of Funds from Liquid Cash Flow and Assets.* The family has the option of paying federal and state death taxes from existing liquid funds and from cash flow capacity, if this would be sufficient to provide adequate funds to pay federal estate taxes

When a family and counsel keep in mind that the tax is due and payable within nine months from the date of death, then the option of funding from cash flow may be of a limited value. If the amount of death taxes is minimal, then this may be an adequate way of handling the payment of death taxes. However, in those situations where a substantial amount of death taxes is due and payable to the federal government and/or a state government, then this may be one of the least attractive and least realistic ways of handling the funding of death taxes.

2. *The Sale of Existing Property of the Estate.* The family has the option of selling estate assets to raise funds to pay death taxes, whether the sale is of real estate or personal property, in many instances the short period of time to pay taxes may result is a sacrifice sale. By way of example, given the real estate market over the last fifteen years, it is clear that on at least two occasions in my practice, there have been substantial delays in being able to sell property at a reasonable price. Often, the family is forced into a sacrifice sale where they must accept substantially less than would be anticipated if they had adequate time to properly market and sell the property.

The other possibility is sale at a profit. Then calculations must be made concerning capital gains taxation when it is necessary to sell either real estate or personal property that will result in net gain.

Also, the sale of existing real or personal property may adversely affect the desires of the beneficiaries regarding distribution of a particular asset. Such a sale may not comport with the representations and desires of the decedent parents, which may have been expressed to the beneficiaries, as to how the assets of the estate are to be divided and distributed.

3. *Borrowing of Funds.* The possibility of the family or legal representative of the estate borrowing funds either from financial institutions or through the government is one option that is available.

The Internal Revenue Code provides for either a discretionary allowance or guaranteed right to extend death taxes over a period of years or a guaranteed right to a particular taxpayer.

This may be a viable alternative provided that the family can feel confident that interest rates will maintain at a reasonable level. But this may not be a possibility. Over the past years as interest rates have varied over a range of 15 percent on an annualized basis, everyone is left with a high degree of uncertainty.

It should also be recognized that interest rates commonly fluctuate quarterly and therefore it cannot be predicted exactly what type of problems are going to be faced.

If the rate was only 9 percent over the period of ten years, the amount actually paid could double the amount due and payable if the funds had been available at the time of the first death. If 22 percent interest had been imposed, then the payment would increase to approximately four times the actual amount due and payable at the nine-month date. This happened in the late 70s.

Similarly, borrowing from financial institutions requires a substantial interest payment and will obviously diminish the amount of liquid assets available for the family for other purposes. This in turn may require the sale of assets, either to pay the interest and/or principal, or to make distributions of cash.

Borrowing funds may be an adequate last resort approach and is one in which there can be substantial flexibility. For example, the government has demonstrated willingness to accept a down payment of a certain amount, with a statutory interest rate imposed, and have the remainder paid over ten years. Although this deferral is generally discretionary, the Internal Revenue Service has tended to be reasonably cooperative.

Also, the government will accept prepayments, which increases the flexibility of available borrowing arrangements.

4. *Utilization of Some Form of a Sinking Fund.* The sinking fund approach may include setting aside funds in various accounts, which are not to be used. This approach appears to have two inherent weaknesses. First, the ultimate amount of taxes due and payable to governmental agencies may be so high that the funds set aside are insufficient. Second, and probably more important, is the reality that if these funds are easily accessible to the

husband and wife, temptation to use them for other purposes may prove too great. The practical economics of family life are such that actual and perceived expenses tend to expand to consume all money available, making this the least attractive of all the options for many people.

Building an Estate and Equalizing Gifts to Children

Life insurance can be used to assist in building an estate for future generations, as well as equalizing gifts, which might otherwise be unequal among the children or other beneficiaries. By way of example, it is uncommon to find that a family may desire one or more children to receive all of the real estate in the estate. Yet, the remaining assets of the estate may be sufficient to equalize the benefits to other children or beneficiaries, and so the family could use an insurance vehicle to bring about equalization.

This technique may have the added benefit that, through an insurance vehicle, it may be possible to have assets owned in a Trust system that is totally non-taxable for death tax purposes.

Particularly in the early years of an individual's or family's estate building efforts, it may be desirable to insure that the size of the estate is increased substantially through the purchase of life insurance products. This will help guard against the effect of an untimely death which would either eliminate or minimize the capacity to build an estate of the size desired to leave to the children or subsequent generations. Life insurance may be the vehicle whereby this is possible. Life insurance is also a way of building an estate through a conservative investment, which is a valid portion of the investment portfolio, having a reasonable return justifying the amount of money that is allocated for the insurance purchase.

As a general proposition, the holding of insurance through an irrevocable trust maximizes the capacity of the family members to develop their planning in such a way as to minimize all forms of taxation. This will ensure that the distribution of the proceeds of insurance is handled in a way that complies with the overall planning technique that has been employed.

Insurance as an Investment

Life insurance can also be justified as part of an investment portfolio for a quality estate plan. Products offered through quality life insurance companies would provide a reasonable return that is tax deferred. Life insurance is a justifiable form of investment, in addition to its usefulness as a method of providing additional funding for the family for whatever reason.

Illustration 14-1 demonstrates a clear comparison among government securities, tax-free municipals, and certificates of deposit versus life insurance.

Illustration 14-1 Life Insurance as an Investment

COMPARISON OF LIFE INSURANCE
AND VARIOUS INVESTMENT ALTERNATIVES

Prepared for: IAN BRIGHT
         Age 35   Male
         Tax Bracket: 28%

Year	Age	Annual Cash Prem Outlay	8% Cert of Deposit	7.75% Money Market Fund	6.5% Tax Free Bond#	7% Annuity-Life Insurance* Liquidity Value##	Account Value	Death Benefit
1	35	1,266	1,339	1,337	1,348	1,321	0	100,000
2	36	1,266	2,755	2,748	2,784	2,701	166	100,000
3	37	1,266	4,253	4,238	4,313	4,143	659	100,815
4	38	1,266	5,836	5,811	5,942	5,653	1,784	101,692
5	39	1,266	7,512	7,472	7,677	7,235	2,947	102,648
6	40	1,266	9,283	9,225	9,524	8,894	4,272	103,695
7	41	1,266	11,157	11,077	11,491	10,636	5,566	104,917
8	42	1,266	13,138	13,032	13,587	12,465	7,136	106,322
9	43	1,266	15,234	15,095	15,818	14,390	8,693	107,910
10	44	1,266	17,450	17,274	18,194	16,415	10,448	109,701
11	45	1,226	19,794	19,575	20,725	18,548	12,477	111,702
12	46	1,266	22,274	22,004	23,421	20,797	15,200	114,152
13	47	1,266	24,895	24,568	26,291	23,169	18,135	117,061
14	48	1,266	27,668	27,276	29,349	25,674	21,402	120,431
15	49	1,266	30,601	30,134	32,605	28,321	24,928	124,226
16	50	1,266	33,702	33,153	36,072	31,119	29,235	128,585
17	51	1,266	36,986	36,339	39,765	34,080	33,433	133,796
18	52	1,266	40,452	39,704	43,698	37,214	38,178	139,205
19	53	1,266	44,121	43,256	47,887	40,534	43,206	145,159
20	54	1,266	48,001	47,006	52,348	44,052	48,758	151,691

21	55	1,266	52,105	50,966	57,099	47,783	54,430	158,839
22	56	1,266	56,445	55,146	62,158	51,742	60,558	166,556
23	57	1,266	61,035	59,560	67,547	55,944	67,203	174,860
24	58	1,266	65,890	64,220	73,286	60,406	74,500	183,700
25	59	1,266	71,024	69,140	79,398	65,148	82,344	193,362

Values include dividends based on the current dividend scale which is neither a projection nor an estimate of future performance. Refer to the underlying illustration proposal for details and guarantees regarding the policy values contained in this illustration.

Life insurance can be a very competitive form of investment. In addition to the investment return, it provides the additional protection that the family may desire for reasons previously discussed. The insurance industry appears to have prevailed with Congress during the 1980s more successfully than any other lobbying group to minimize the increases in real taxation that generally have been imposed across the board on individuals and institutions within the American economy.

The earnings on the investment fund of an individual's policy, commonly known as *cash value*, are allowed to accumulate on a tax-deferred basis. The effect of this is that so long as the policy is not surrendered during the life of the individual, all of those funds, which are allocated to the cash value portion of the life of the life insurance policy, are allowed to earn on a tax-deferred basis, and forgiven if held until the death of the insured.

Problem of Taxation of Life Insurance

The entire subject of the taxation of life insurance may be one of the most complex issues connected with the United States tax system, for two reasons.

First, the Internal Revenue Service appears to have an inherent dislike for any insurance proceeds that are not taxed along with decedent's estate assets. The reason for this irrational position is not clear, but this fact is known to all that are familiar with the subject. Second, the case law over many years has been so diverse and inconsistent concerning the concept of incidents of ownership that unless planning is carefully done with counsel, financial planners, and underwriters who understand their subject, the possibility of life insurance proceeds ending up taxed is highly probable.

In fact, my experience in more than thirty-seven years of legal practice has demonstrated that in as much as 90 percent of cases, whether because of the way in which the insurance policy was applied for, owned, or paid for, life insurance has been included in an individual's estate and death taxes imposed.

Unfortunately, part of the problem is the tragic lack of understanding that the insurance industry has of the system. Some of the informational bulletins read by the author concerning community property state law coming from East Coast insurance companies are often inaccurate. It is amazing that more litigation has not arisen against insurance companies for their failure to research this subject more thoroughly and provide proper education to their field force and administrative personnel. Also, the fact that three-year contemplation of death statutes are applicable to life insurance products makes it even more important to analyze how life insurance is purchased.

An irrevocable trust that is created properly and funded in a way that complies with the law (provided reporting is done carefully and consistently) ensures that life insurance proceeds will not be included in an individual's estate. It is only through the use of trusts that the maximum tax benefits can be realized. Therefore, it is important to review basic elements of the trust concept and the eight basic elements of the purchase and implementation of a life insurance policy is as follows:

1. The applicant
2. The owner
3. The contingent owner if the owner dies before the insured
4. The premium payer
5. The insured
6. The beneficiary
7. The contingent beneficiary
8. The residual control held by the insured(s)
   (Sometimes referred to as incidents of ownership)

The eight elements must be understood by your planner. If they do not understand them, or will not learn them, find a different attorney.

Description of a Trust

Since trusts are so vital as a tool to minimize taxes in the estate planning process when life insurance is purchased, it is important to have a basic understanding of the elements of a trust and the unique way in which trusts function.

The four basic elements of a trust include
1. *Trustor* (also referred to as *settlor* and *grantor*) - the individual(s) who brings the trust into existence
2. *Trustee* - the manager of the trust
3. *Beneficiary(ies)* - those who are to receive the benefits of the trusts as to either income and/or principal
4. *Res* (also referred to as corpus of principal) - the assets which are placed into the trust

Trusts can be in any of four categories, which are:

1. The testamentary revocable trust
2. A testamentary irrevocable trust
3. A living revocable trust
4. A living irrevocable trust

The first two types of trusts are brought into existence through a will and the second two are brought into existence during lifetime, hence the terminology "living trust." In understanding trusts, it is helpful to understand ownership of property under the common law prior to the common existence of trusts compared to ownership of property under a trust as it developed under the common law.

Initially, property was held by an individual in his own name. This person had full use of the property and hence owned both legal title and beneficial title as demonstrated in Illustration 14-2. This type of ownership was referred to as a fee simple absolute, and this is still the basic way in which property is owned in those countries that derive their law from the historical common law. A trust, however, is an arrangement that divides the ownership rights of legal ownership and beneficial ownership into two parallel levels of ownership.

Illustration 14-2 Basic Trust Conceptual Diagram

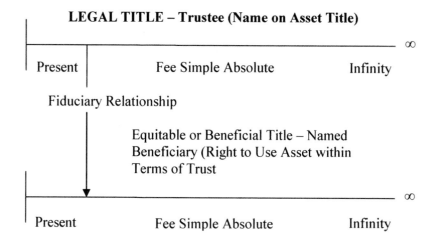

Various Kinds of Trusts for Insurance Purchase

There are at least seven types of trusts that could act as the owner of a life insurance product:

1. A family credit by-pass trust (A-B trust)
2. Dry trust (unfunded)
3. Trust with minimum assets where dry trusts are not allowed
4. Crummey trust
5. Internal Revenue Code Section 2503(c) trust
6. Internal Revenue Code Section 2503 (b) trust
7. Contingent owner trust

In the purchase of life insurance, all trusts have four elements in common, which include:

1. All are irrevocable
2. Each provides a method whereby the insurance proceeds may be kept out of the estate of the insured for federal estate death tax and state inheritance tax.
3. Each trust has been brought into existence by historical case law, such as the Crummey trust or statutory trust, brought into

       existence by specific sections of the Internal Revenue Code, such as IRC 2503

4. Each of these trusts are not required to own or purchase life insurance, but under most circumstances would have the authority to either receive life insurance or act as the legal entity to purchase life insurance on any particular individual

It has been suggested that the various kinds of life insurance are products that the internal Revenue Service would prefer to tax. As a consequence, it is recommended that those involved in the estate planning process recognize that utilization of words and headings of trusts may have a significant effect on how the taxation is imposed.

In conjunction with the type of analysis, a plea is made that the term insurance trust not be used. In fact, there is no such thing as an insurance trust. What exists is either a revocable trust or an irrevocable trust, which has the authority to purchase life insurance. By utilizing proper nomenclature in the description of the estate planning vehicles, it is possible to set the proper tone for minimizing undesirable taxation.

The Amount of Insurance Needed

Probably the only accurate statement about how much insurance is needed is that no one really knows. This is probably the most subjective area in the entire analysis. However, it is suggested that an understanding of the following facts about any particular family or business as well as their desires, both during the present and in the future are particularly relevant.

1. Family expenses
2. Debt service
3. Pay-off desires in the event of death
4. Business requirements and needs
5. Death taxes of all kinds
6. Wealth accumulation during retirement years
7. Wealth accumulation after the death of one spouse

8. Actual wealth at the present time
9. Financial needs today versus needs in the future

Creditor Protection Arrangement Possibilities with Life Insurance

With the increasingly litigious nature of American society, there are some interesting possibilities for utilizing life insurance vehicles to protect the economic welfare of the family. Illustration 14-3 outlines, in detail, the way the breadwinner of a family may be an insured person with the policy being applied for, owned, and paid for by the other spouse and managed in such a way so as to ensure that in the event of the death of the breadwinner, the proceeds of the life insurance policy will be held secure from invasion of creditors of any kind.

In analyzing the various aspects of Illustration 14-3, it should be realized that there is great precision in both the sequence of events and the preparation of documents that are fundamental to the success of the entire arrangement. An earnest plea is made that if use is to be made of this arrangement, that it be analyzed thoroughly and followed meticulously.

Illustration 14-3 Wife's Irrevocable Trust

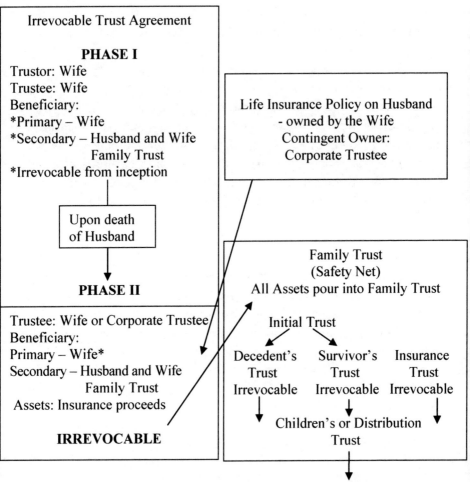

*Wife's Rights in Trust
a. Life estate as to income and use of all property.
b. Invasion of principal for ascertainable standards.
c. Invasion annually of principal for any purpose up to 5 percent or $5,000, whichever is greater

Note: Are There Limitations Imposed Upon the Wife?
Functionally, the wife has full use of all income and principal—except for the right to waste or gift away the assets of the trust.

Basic Assumptions

1. Husband and wife hold property as tenants in common or as community property when the residence is in a community property state
2. Husband is primary income producer
3. Possibility of liability against husband by virtue of professional exposure
4. Reverse could be true if wife were the primary source of income
5. The family has in existence basic credit by-pass trust, or preparation is in process
6. State law will allow an unfunded (dry) trust; if not, then minimal funding can be used
7. Husband dies
8. All arrangements in writing

Critical Elements in the Insuring Process

Insures:	Husband
Applicant:	Wife
Owner:	Wife, as her sole and separate property
Contingent Owner:	Corporate trustee or independent trustee
Beneficiary:	Wife's irrevocable trust
Contingent Beneficiary:	If primary beneficiary dies, name alternate
Premium Payor:	Wife from sole and separate property bank account created by contract

Residual control not held by the insured husband.

Sequence of Events

1. Creation of the irrevocable insurance trust agreement
2. Death of husband activates phase II

3.   Payment of policy proceeds to trustee
4.   Use of insurance proceeds by wife as primary beneficiary
5.   Death of wife activates transfer of irrevocable trust funds to family trust
6.   Use and distribution of all family assets to beneficiaries

Necessary Bank Account System

If it is desired to be very conservative in an attempt to guarantee that the life insurance proceeds will not be taxed, it is recommended that a formal separation of funds be accomplished by contract and by separate bank accounts (see Illustration 14-4). This is to be established by contract to protect wife from liabilities and claims against husband.

Illustration 14-4 Necessary Bank Accounts System

This is to be established by contract to protect Wife from liabilities and claims against Husband

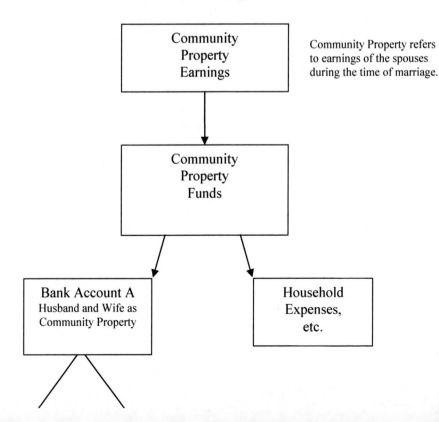

Community Property Earnings

Community Property refers to earnings of the spouses during the time of marriage.

Community Property Funds

Bank Account A
Husband and Wife as Community Property

Household Expenses, etc.

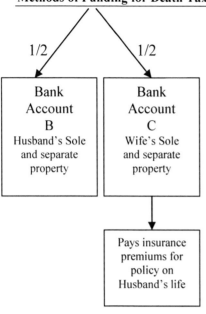

1. Account A functions as a pass-through to divide Community Property funds.
2. Accounts B and C must be funded equally.
3. Accounts B and C may be used independently and are not required to maintain equal balances.
4. Account B funds may be used for any purpose except for premium payments on husband's insurance.
5. Only bank account minimum balances are required in each account.

Charitable Giving with Life Insurance

There are a number of ways in which life insurance can be used as a vehicle to transfer funds to a charitable institution. Which of these are chosen depends on the goals and economic capacity of the family. There are at least three commonly used arrangements:

In one arrangement, the policy is owned by the insured or other members of the family, where a charitable institution is the direct beneficiary. This would clearly be deductible for federal estate tax purposes and for state inheritance tax purposes.

On occasion, charitable institutions have been wise enough to realize that their long-term fund-raising is well served by allowing an individual to make contributions to the institution and allow the institution to be the applicant owner and premium payor of an insurance policy on the donor's life. Although there may be some arguments that could be made under some circumstances that there is not an insurable interest, the practical experience of the author dictates that insurance companies seldom raise this as a primary issue. However, the use of an irrevocable trust can eliminate the problem.

Where the charitable institution has been far sighted enough to see the wisdom of this approach, they provide the opportunity for the insured to make a contribution for which there is a present deduction against income taxes by the donor. The opportunity of having funds accumulate during the remainder of the life of the insured, and the opportunity of the donor knowing that a substantial amount of funds which may be far in excess of the donor's capacity to donate in any other way is eventually going to be received by the charitable institution.

Finally, a number of types of trusts may be utilized in the purchase of life insurance wherein either the life insurance proceeds are used to provide a donation to the charitable institution, or life insurance proceeds are used as a method by which the funds which are being gifted to the charitable institution can be returned to the family upon the death of the insured.

Illustration 14-5 demonstrates the method by which a very simple charitable remainder trust is created. This is a trust arrangement by which the donor(s) gift a certain sum of money and/or property with a known value to a charitable institution. In return, they receive an annual income property with a known value to a charitable institution. In return, the donor receives an annual income equal to a fixed percentage or an amount that represents the entire income earned by the property that has been transferred to the charitable institution. Under both circumstances, that amount received may not be less than 5 percent.

Illustration 14-5 Charitable Remainder Annuity Trust in the form of an Annuity Trust*

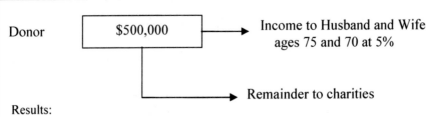

Results:
1. Income tax deduction here is $240,000 approximately.
   (This commonly changes)
2. Annuity payment is $35,000/year no matter the value of the corpus.
3. If the annuity payment is deemed under the IRS' probability test to bear a chance greater than 5% of exhausting the trust assets, no deduction is allowed.

Amount to be paid – SMALLER of trust income or unitrust amount, i.e. no minimum 5%.

OR

Number (1) above PLUS trust income in excess of unitrust amount to the extent that actual trust income in prior years (accumulated) was less than the unitrust amounts (accumulated).

Other Pertinent Assumptions:
1. Donative Intent Exists
2. Trustee is Independent of Donor
3. Irrevocable

*The Charitable Remainder Unit Trust would be diagrammed the same way

Illustration 14-6 shows a method whereby the income received from the charitable institution can be used through another trust arrangement to purchase life insurance. The proceeds would be paid outside of the insured's estate and hence, allow for a restoration to the family of the wealth transferred to the charitable institution. This particular approach is becoming progressively more popular and is one in which it appears that both the family and the charitable institution maximize their capacity to both give and retain wealth at the same time.

Illustration 14-6 Wealth Restoration

Example of Restoring Wealth to Your Family

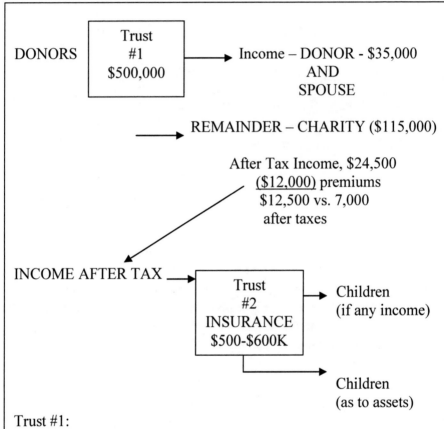

Trust #1:
(1) Increased income to donors
(2) Gift to charity
(3) Other benefits

Trust #2:
(1) Transfer to trust within annual exclusion (no gift tax limits).
(2) Policy value replaces gift made to charity.
(3) No estate tax, no income tax, no probate. (Remember the *trustee* must be independent from family and must initiate the policy purchases to avoid incidents of ownership in parents.)

Other Pertinent Assumptions:

(1) Donative Intent Exists
(2) Trustees are Independent of Donors
(3) Both Trusts Irrevocable

Summary

The utilization of life insurance with a trust as a primary funding vehicle for federal estate taxes and state inheritance taxes is one of the most efficient and useful estate planning techniques available within the United States' economic system. Its effective use requires the concerted efforts of not only the purchaser of the insurance, but also professional advisors, including life underwriters, attorneys, financial planners, and accountants. Without a full team approach, full success in this is unlikely. With careful planning and implementation of trusts and life insurance, the benefits may be uniquely effective for any family.

15

Revocable Trusts and Powers of Attorney for Health Care for the Disabled

Incomplete Perception

Too often, there is a general perception that the use of a trust is primarily for transfer of assets at the time of death to avoid probate: second, as a vehicle to maximize tax savings through the use of a traditional A-B trust.

It would certainly be inappropriate to, in any way, minimize the value of a trust for those purposes and, in fact, they should be consistently promoted and utilized for those very purposes.

The More Important Purpose of Living Trusts and Durable Powers of Attorney for Health Care

However, there is a far more important reason in the utilization of a trust combined with a durable power of attorney for health care, than to act as a vehicle for avoidance of probate and maximizing tax savings.

The most important utilization in the mind of this writer is the use of the revocable living trust along with a durable power of attorney for health care for those who have become disabled. This may be an unusual disability problem that has come on fairly early, as was described in Chapter 5 with my sister. More than likely, there will be a scenario that comes about by simply the advanced age of an individual who is no longer physically, and perhaps even mentally, able to manage their own affairs either in terms of directing medical services, or in the management of money.

With a revocable living trust, the successor trustee takes over at the time of disability (that may be permanent in nature), and provides an enormous amount of savings of the estate funds as well as maximizing the maintenance of the dignity of the individual.

It is not a very difficult observation to make by walking down the halls of any assisted living facility for the elderly to see many people who have obviously lost their capacity to have meaningful cognitive processes, and whose physical capacities are so debilitated, that but for the assisted living care, they would not be able to continue any kind of normal existence.

For example, in assisted living facilities, there have commonly been three divisions. The first is designed for those who are completely ambulatory and are able to fix their own meals, and live in an apartment-type condition. However, normally combined with that is the availability of a cafeteria in case the individual on any particular day may not want to fix his or her own meal.

The second level is for those who are no longer able to handle even the fixing of meals, but are not in need of continual medical services. This is becoming progressively more common throughout the country. This second level has grown immensely in the last decade. The reason for this seems to be a very practical one. As an individual grows older, even if they are able to handle their meals, the practical reality of trying to maintain cleanliness of their living facility and the maintenance of a home or a large apartment becomes progressively prohibitive.

The third level is where there is serious medical treatment and care needed, and hence, it is functionally a form of a hospital designed for permanent residency.

Having worked with all three of these levels of care, and particularly those with the three within the same facility, they appear to become progressively more helpful to the person being assisted and one which families can be proud to have an elderly member of the family use as a living facility during their final years or even days.

Deciding on the Trustee and the Agent

In using this kind of arrangement, it appears that the two most important decisions that an individual needs to make has to do with finding an individual who you are going to trust, someone to make medical care decisions on your behalf. This is the primary function of a power of attorney for health care.

Second is the choice of a successor trustee. Of necessity, this must be an individual of integrity and hopefully, to the extent possible, the person who has maximum experience in the management of investments and developing budgets by which an individual can survive in an assisted living facility. Experience has shown that this can be very difficult.

A Court Controlled Conservatorship

The alternative to this kind of arrangement has been previously discussed in this book. However, by way of review, the only alternative where there is not a living will declaration accompanied with a durable power of attorney for health care, and an individual becomes seriously disabled, is the utilization of the courts in overseeing some form of conservatorship. By way of review, the cost of even establishing a court-controlled conservatorship during the first year will range between $7,000 and commonly as much as $12,000.

However, far more important than the finances of the arrangement, is the demeaning effect of requiring individuals who are disabled or progressively in a debilitating condition to appear before an open court so the judge can look down on them and say, "Yup, you are not nuts and we are going to take over your life.

If this seems rude or crude in terms of how it functions, it is suggested that only the words have changed. The reality of having individuals brought into open court during their disability or old age is never less than embarrassing. The judge will not use crude language, but it is always demeaning.

There are times when it is absolutely ridiculous. By way of example, this past year the court required an individual who was nearly comatose to literally be brought into the court on a gurney, since the diagnosis was serious and the only perceived care that could be rendered that would be meaningful was shock treatment.

To have a non-medical person acting as a judge looking down on this poor lady as if they had the capacity to know whether it was appropriate to have shock treatment or not borders on the ridiculous.

There is certainly no reason why this system could not be properly managed by having a certification by a court-appointed doctor to make the determination whether the diagnosis and recommended treatment was valid. The requirement of having such a person appear in court is beyond the comprehension of this writer and lawyer.

Summary

In summation, the management of money, the direction of medical treatment and allowing an individual to maximize their dignity during their entire life seem to be very worthy objectives, and those vehicles that are available to maximize one's ability to maintain dignity seem to be the appropriate ones to be chosen.

16

Frequently Asked Questions

Q: Must a will be probated?

A: Yes! A will, by definition, is a legal document that does not become effective as a will until it is submitted to a probate court with a petition accompanied by a signed copy of the will, at which time the court determines whether it qualifies as a valid will or not. From that point forward it must go through a fairly rigorous procedure, to pay for appraisals and payment of creditors as well as other technical requirements.

The probate is inherently complicated and often very confusing and can also be quite costly. As a rule of thumb, it should be assumed by way of many studies over the years, the cost of probate is approximately $35,000 for every $500,000 of assets and $64,000 for every $1 million of assets. (See Chapter 3 and Appendix B)

Q: Does a revocable trust require probate?

A: A revocable trust does not need to be probated if all assets have been transferred to the name of the trust. (See Chapters 5 and 6 and Appendix A)

Q: What is the difference between a will and a trust?

A: The distinction between a trust and a will, is that a trust is a private legal instrument signed by the creator of the trust (trustor and/or settlers) and the trustee(s), or manager(s), wherein they (trustor) are the initial beneficiaries. The arrangement is not subject to probate of the asset being transferred to the trust. In contrast, the will is a document that, as a matter of law, must be subject to the probate court. It should be assumed that the settlement of the estate should not take less than a year and a half, and can take up to two years to settle. (See Chapter 7)

Q: When should I get a will or trust?

A: Individuals have to be very practical about answering the question of when they should have a will or trust.

As a general proposition, it is suggested to young couples that have just been married, that it may be sufficient for them to hold property and joint tenancy with only a will.

However, it is recommended that once there are children, the considerations are very different and the trust has significant value.

It is also the fact that as individuals become older, it is wiser to use a trust versus the will because the likelihood of death increases significantly as one exceeds the age of fifty.

Q: I have a small estate, is a trust of value to me?

A: Although your estate may be small, the issue of whether or not a trust is of value to you should be analyzed in two elements. First, you have no guarantee that you will not become disabled. If you are disabled and the assets are in the trust, then it can be managed privately without the introduction of the probate court, through a conservatorship. On the other hand, if there is a conservatorship imposed and the assets have not been transferred to the trust, then it will be subject to the rigors of court administration and large costs involved with the establishment, management, administration, and accounting of the conservatorship.

The cost of the relatively small estate can be substantial. Experience has demonstrated that estates as small as $300,000 going through probate can commonly rise to a high level. Part of the reason for this is that an estate that is being probated is measured by the gross value of the real estate, and not upon equity. Therefore, the use of a trust can produce a significant savings during life, and at the time of death. In addition, the trust maximizes privacy opposed to the assets that are passed through the probate system, where it is readily available to all members of the public. (See Chapter 3.02)

Q: What is required to update a will or trust?

A: As a matter of practice, one has to recognize that during their lifetime, such as at the time of marriage, there will be many changes that take place in both the economic condition and the size of the family. The general recommendation is that the trust and will should be reexamined not less than every three years by the individual's family's attorney and/or more frequently if there are unusual circumstances that have taken place which require modification of a demonstration of the family's desires. In the event of a serious illness or accident, it would be appropriate to have a "special needs trust" drafted through a qualified attorney.

Q: Does a revocable trust protect a person from creditors?

A: The answer is a resounding No. It is tragic that there had been too many articles and promotions by individuals, who should be ashamed of themselves, who claim a revocable trust will protect you from creditors. In a very real sense, a revocable trust is simply a will substitute, and does not, for all practical purposes, come into existence until that individual dies and/or one of the spouses of the marriage dies.

Prior to the death of either spouse or the individual, a revocable trust does not protect anyone from creditors. (See Chapter 9)

Q: What is an advanced directive?

A: An advanced directive is a legal document wherein an individual authorizes a particular person to act on their behalf in directing medical services. This is referred to as a "power of attorney for health care." This can be as broad or as limited as a person desires. All states provide for the use of the advanced directive. As an arrangement that has greatly allowed for much more efficiency in caring for individuals in what may be a crisis situation, like an automobile crash. Without an advanced directive, it may be necessary to apply to a court for the establishment of a conservatorship, when the same services can be rendered much easier and with much less expense with the use of an advanced directive. (See Chapter 15 and Appendix C)

Q: What is a living will declaration?

A: A living will declaration is a legal document that has been adopted by most states. It is a poorly named vehicle. In fact, it is simply too euphemistic. It would be far more correct to refer to this document as a "directive to physicians." Its function is to express an individual's wishes, that in the event they have reached a point of no return in their health, and death is imminent, and two doctors agree that such is the case, that they are directed to withdraw life support, so as to simply not maintain the technical legal existence of the individual who has functionally passed away. This is also sometimes referred to as a "do not resuscitate" arrangement, but that seems a little crude.

Sometimes the living will declaration is combined with the durable power of attorney for health care," the issues are very different and is not recommended. (See Chapter 7 and Appendices D, E, and F)

Q: What kind of written instructions do I need to manage a trust?

A: The kind of information by way of instructions that should be provided to you by the attorney drafting the trust on your behalf, dictates that you should be given a formal letter indicating the name of the trust, and an explanation of what should be done with various kinds of assets. Examination of Appendix H demonstrates the information indicating the name of the trust as well as the table of contents indicating that kind of information that you should receive in those letters of instructions to properly administer the trust during your life, and for the successor trustee to administer the trust upon your passing. (See Chapter 13 and Appendix H)

GLOSSARY

Adjusted Gross Estate—For federal estate tax purposes, the *gross estate* minus certain allowed deductions.

Administration—The care and management of an estate by an executor, an administrator, a trustee or a guardian.

Administrator with Will Annexed (abbreviated to Administrator C.T.A.)—An individual or trust institution appointed by a court to settle the estate of a deceased person in accordance with the terms of that person's will when no executor has been named in the will or when one named has failed to qualify.

After-Born Child—A child born after the execution of the parent's will.

Ancestor—One who precedes another in the line of descent; In common law, the term ancestor applied only to a person in the direct line of ascent—father, grandfather, or other forebear—but by statute it has been broadened to apply also to a person of collateral relationship—as in uncle or aunt—from whom property has been acquired.

Annual Exclusion—A gift tax exclusion allowing a donor to annually make gifts of $10,000 per donee. There are no limits to the number of donees.

Annuity—A stated amount payable annually or at other regular intervals for either a certain and/or indefinite period, as for a stated number of years or for life.

Antenuptial—Before marriage.

Attestation Clause—The clause of a document containing the formal declaration of the act of witnessing; in the case of a will, the clause immediately following the signature of the testator and usually beginning, "Signed, sealed, published, and declared by the said..."

Attorney-in-Fact—A person who, as agent, is given written authorization by another person to transact business for his or her principal out of court.

Basis—In tax law, the amount representing original cost plus cost of improvements, which is used in calculating capital gain.

Beneficiary—(1) The person for whose benefit a trust is created. (2) The person to whom the amount of an insurance policy or annuity is payable.

Bequest—A testamentary gift of personal property. The term has sometimes been held to include real property also.

Bond—A sum to be posted either in cash or through a bonding company to ensure performance by the legal representative of an estate, whether executor, administrator, or trustee.

Buy-Sell Agreement—A contract commonly used in partnerships and closely held corporations wherein the corporation and/or the other stockholders agree to purchase the stock of a decedent stockholder. These agreements fall into two categories: (1) a stock redemption program wherein the corporation repurchases the stock, and (2) a cross-purchase agreement wherein the existing stockholders purchase the stock of the decedent stockholder.

Charitable Bequest—A gift of personal property to a charity by will.

Charitable Devise—A gift of real property to a charity by will.

Charity—A gift of real or personal property, or both, to be applied, consistently with existing laws, for the benefit of an indefinite number of persons by bringing their hearts under the influence of education or religion; by relieving their bodies from disease, suffering, or constraint; by assisting them to establish themselves in life; or by creating or maintaining public buildings or works, or otherwise lessening the burden of government.

Chattel—Any property, movable or immovable, except a freehold estate in land.

Clifford Trust—A short-term irrevocable trust, which lasts at least ten years. When the trust ends, the principal is returned to the trustor.

Codicil—An amendment or supplement to a will. It must be executed with all the formalities of the will itself.

Community Property—Property in which a husband and wife each have an undivided one-half interest by reason of their marital status; recognized in all civil law countries and in certain states of the southwest and Pacific coast areas of the United States, including Washington, California, Nevada, Arizona, New Mexico, Texas, Louisiana and Idaho.

Competent—Legally qualified; possessing adequate mental capacity.

Contest of Will—An attempt by legal process to prevent the probate of a will or the distribution of property according to the will.

Corporate Fiduciary—A trust institution serving in a fiduciary capacity, such as executor, administrator, trustee, or guardian.

Corporate Trustee—A trust institution serving as trustee.

Corpus—The principal or capital of an estate as distinguished from the income.

Credit By-Pass Trust—A trust whereby decedent spouse leaves the maximum of equivalent estate tax exemption irrevocably in a life estate to the surviving spouse.

Curtesy—The interest or life estate of a widower in the real property of his wife who died without leaving a valid will or from whose will he has dissented. At common law, curtesy took effect only if a child capable of inheriting the property had been born of the marriage. In many states, common law curtesy has been abolished by statute or has never been recognized.

Death Taxes—Taxes imposed on property or on the transfer of property at the owner's death; a general term covering estate taxes as well as other succession or transfer taxes.

Decedent—A deceased person.

Descendent—One who is descended in a direct line from another, however remotely; the same as *issue*.

Devise—A gift of real property by will. A person who receives such a gift is called a *devisee*.

Disclaimer—An unqualified refusal by persons to accept an interest in property when another has attempted to gift such a property to them, generally effective provided that the disclaimer is in writing and delivered on a timely basis to an estate legal representative.

Discretionary Trust—A trust that entitles the beneficiary only to so much of the income or principal as the trustee, in its uncontrolled discretion, shall see fit to give the beneficiary or apply for his or her use.

Distribution—In law, the appointment by a court of the personal property of one who died intestate among those entitled to receive the property, according to a particular state's applicable statute concerning distribution; to be distinguished from *disbursement*.

Domicile—The place where a person has his or her permanent home and principal establishment; the place to which, whenever the person is absent, he or she has the intention of returning. A person's domicile may or may not be the same as his or her residence at a given time.

Donee—The person to whom a gift is made.

Donor—A person who makes a gift.

Dower—The interest or life estate of a widow in the real property of her husband. At common law, a wife had a life estate in one-third of the real property of her husband who died without leaving a valid will or from whose will she dissented.

Dry Trust—A trust without assets.

Duress—A compulsion or constraint by force or fear of personal violence, prosecution, or imprisonment, which induces a person to do what he or she does not want to do or to refrain from doing something he or she has a legal right to do. Sometimes the word is used with reference to the making of a will, as that it was made under duress.

Election Against the Will—The option provided by many states for a widow or widower to take a specified portion of the spouse's estate in lieu of a bequest contained in the deceased spouse's will.

Equitable Ownership—The estate or interest of a person who has a beneficial right in property, the legal ownership of which is in another person. A beneficiary of a trust has an equitable estate or interest in the trust property.

Equitable Title—A right to the benefits of property, which is recognized by and enforceable only in a court of equity; to be distinguished from *legal title.*

Escheat—The reversion of property to the state, in the United States, in case there are no devisees, legatees, heirs, or next of kin; originally applicable only to real property, but now applicable to all kinds of property.

Estate—(1) The right, title, or interest, which a person has in any property; to be distinguished from the property itself; which is the subject matter of the interest. (2) The property of descent.

Estate Tax—A tax imposed upon a decedent's estate, as such, and not on the distributive shares of the estate or on the right to receive the shares.

Executor—An individual or trust institution nominated in a will and appointed by a court to settle the estate of the testator. If a woman is nominated and appointed, she is known as an *executrix.* Also known as the legal representative.

Executrix—A woman appointed as a legal representative.

Fee Simple (Fee Simple Absolute) —An absolute fee, that is, an estate of inheritance without limitation to any particular class of heirs and with no restrictions upon alienation; sometimes known as *fee simple absolute;* the largest estate a person may own.

Fiduciary—An individual or a trust institution charged with the duty of acting for the benefit of another party as to matters coming within the scope of the relationship between them.

Flower Bond—An issue of low-yielding United States Treasury bonds, which are purchased at a discount and are redeemable at face value upon the owner's death to pay estate taxes.

Future Interest—An interest in property—either personal or real—which can only be enjoyed at a future date.

Generation-Skipping Transfer Tax (GSTT)—Federal tax on transfers in trust form, or its equivalent, which pass from one generation to successive generations.

Gift—A gratuitous, voluntary transfer of property. A gift requires two elements, which are: (1) an intent of the donor to make a gift, and (2) the actual delivery of the property to the intended donee.

Grantor—A person who transfers property by deed or who grants property rights by means of a trust instrument or some other document.

Grantor Trust—A trust over which the grantor retains such a degree of control that the trust property is considered to belong to the grantor. The grantor must generally pay income taxes on the income the trust earns.

Gross Estate—The sum total of an individual's property for estate tax purposes.

Guardian—An individual or a trust institution appointed by a court to care for the property or the person, or both, of a minor or an incompetent. When the guardian's duties are limited to the property, he or she is known as a *guardian of the property;* when they are limited to the person, he or she is known as the *guardian of the person;* when they apply to both the property and the person, he or she is known merely as *guardian.* In some states, the term *committee, conservator,* or *tutor* is used to designate one who performs essentially the same duties as a guardian.

Heir—A person who inherits real property. An heir of the body is an heir in the direct line of the decedent.

Holographic Will—An instrument identified by three elements, namely: (1) It is wholly in the handwriting of the testator; (2) It is signed by the testator; (3) It is dated by the testator. Some jurisdictions limit the validity of holographic wills, and the procedural requirements are rigidly enforced.

Incidents of Ownership—An interest of an individual in a life insurance policy, the effect of which will cause the policy to be treated as belonging to that individual for tax purposes.

Inheritance Tax—A tax imposed after administration costs and estate taxes on the right to receive property by inheritance.

Insurance Trust—A trust composed partly or wholly of life insurance policy contracts.

Intangible Property—Property that cannot be touched or realized with the senses, such as a legally enforceable right. The right possessed by the holder of a promissory note or bond is intangible property, the paper and writing being the only evidences of that right.

Inter Vivos—Between living persons; in the term of *trust inter vivos* or *inter vivos trust,* the same as a living trust.

Intestacy—The condition resulting from a person's dying without leaving a valid will.

Invasion of Trust—A distribution made from the principal of a trust created either during lifetime or by will. Invasion rights are normally designated by the creator of a trust or a testamentary instrument.

Irrevocable Trust—A trust, which, by its terms, cannot be revoked by the settlor or trustor.

Issue—All persons who have descended from a common ancestor; a broader term than *children.*

Joint Tenancy—The holding of property by two or more persons in such a manner that, upon the death of one joint owner, the survivor or survivors take the entire property.

Jurat—A certificate evidencing the fact that an affidavit was properly made before a duly authorized officer.

Last Will—The will last executed by a person. Since all former wills ordinarily are revoked by the last one, the term is used to emphasize the fact that it is the latest and, therefore, the effective will of the maker.

Laws of Descent—Laws governing the descent of real property from ancestor to heir.

Legal Ownership—An estate or interest in property, which is enforceable in a court of law.

Legal Title—Title to property recognized by and enforceable in a court of law.

Legatee—One to whom personal property is bequeathed in a will.

Letters Testamentary—A certificate of authority to settle a particular estate issued to an executor by the appointing court.

Life Estate—Either an estate for the life of the tenant alone, or an estate for the life or lives of some person or persons other than the tenant.

Living Trust—A trust that becomes operative during the lifetime of the settlor or trustor, as opposed to a trust under will. The same as a *trust inter vivos*. Such a trust may be revocable or irrevocable.

Marital Deduction—The value of property that is deducted from the taxable estate of a decedent spouse and passed to the surviving spouse in fee or within the parameters of Internal Revenue Code Section 2056.[9]

Merger—Historically, under the law of merger, if the same individual became both the trustee and the beneficiary, there was a merger of interest, and the trust went out of existence. In the majority of states within the United States, this no longer applies. However, New York is a notable exception.

Net Income—A person's income after expenses are paid.

Net Worth—The value of a person's assets minus his or her liabilities.

Per Stirpes—A term used in the distribution of property; distribution to persons as members of a family (per stirpes) and not as individuals (per capita). Two or more children of the same parent

---

[9] I.R.C. §2056 (1997).

take per stirpes when together they take what the parent, if living, would take.

Power—Authority or right to do or refrain from doing a particular act, as a trustee's power of sale or power to withhold income; to be distinguished from *trust powers.*

Power of Appointment—A right given to a person to dispose of property that he or she does not own. A power of appointment may be general or special. Under a *general* power, the donee may exercise the right as he or she sees fit. A *special* power limits the donee as to those in favor of whom he or she may exercise the power of appointment. For example, a wife who is given the power to appoint among her children has a special power of appointment.

Power of Attorney—A document, witnessed and acknowledged, authorizing the person named therein to act as *attorney-in-fact* for the person signing the document. If the attorney-in-fact is authorized to act for his or her principal in all matters, he or she has a *general power of attorney;* if he or she has authority to do only special things, he or she has a *special power of attorney.* In financial transactions, the power of attorney is usually special.

Principal—(1) In either a trust or a will, the real and personal property that initially makes up the corpus of the estate or that is subsequently transferred thereto, from which income is produced. (2) In an agency relationship, the principal is the individual who authorizes another individual, known as an agent, to act on his or her behalf.

Probate—The system whereby a court of common jurisdiction takes authority over the assets of the estate of an individual and determines the validity of a will and appoints a legal representative to manage the affairs under the jurisdiction of the court.

Prudent Person Rule for Trust Investment—A term applied to a rule laid down by statute or by judicial decision, which authorizes a fiduciary to apply the standard of a prudent investor, instead of selecting investments according to a list prescribed by statutes or by some governmental agency under authority of law; formerly known as the *American Rule* or the *Massachusetts Rule.* Historically known as the *Prudent Man Rule.*

Qualified Terminable Interest Property—A type of trust interest in property passed from one spouse to the other, which qualifies for an estate tax marital deduction only if (1) the surviving spouse will receive the income from the property, payable annually, for the duration of his or her life; and (2) no person has the power to appoint the property to anyone other than the surviving spouse.

Q-TIP—Abbreviation for qualified terminable interest property

Remainder—A future estate in real property, which will become an estate in possession upon the termination of the prior estate created at the same time and by the same instrument as the future estate.

Residence—The place where one resides, whether temporarily or permanently.

Reversion—The interest in an estate remaining in the grantor after a particular interest, less than the whole estate, has been granted by the owner to another person. The reversion remains in the grantor; the remainder goes to some grantee.

Revocable Trust—A trust that, by its terms, may be terminated by the settlor or trustor or by another person.

Rule Against Perpetuities—A rule of common law that makes void any estate or interest in property so limited that it will not take effect or *vest* within a period measured by a life or lives in being at the time of creation of the estate plus twenty-one years. This is being changed in many states.

Situs—Location.

Spendthrift Provision—A provision in a trust instrument that limits the right of the beneficiary to dispose of his or her interest, as by assignment, and the right of the beneficiary's creditors to reach it, as by attachment.

Sprinkling Clause—Discretion given to a trustee in the distribution of income from the trust. Such power must be provided for in the trust assignment.

Statute of Wills—Statutes providing that no will shall be valid, and no devise or bequest shall be valid unless the will is in writing, signed, and attested in the manner provided by the statute.

Subscribing Witness—One who sees a document signed or hears the signature acknowledged by the signor and who signs his or her own name to the document, such as the subscribing witness to a will.

Successor Trustee—A trustee following the original or a prior trustee, the appointment of whom is provided for in the trust instrument.

Tenancy—The holding of property by any form of title.

Tenancy by the Entirety—Tenancy by a husband or wife in such a manner that, except in concert with the other, neither husband nor wife has a disposable interest in the property during the lifetime of the other. Upon the death of either, the property goes to the survivor.

Testamentary Capacity—The legal capability imposed by law that determines whether an individual has the legal capacity to sign a testamentary instrument. Historically, an individual was deemed competent to execute a testamentary instrument provided he or she could recognize the natural object of his or her affection.

Testamentary Trust—A trust established by a will, which comes into existence at the end of probate.

Three-Year Contemplation-of-Death Statute—The Internal Revenue Code now specifically provides that, as it applies to life insurance only, that if such insurance is purchased within three years prior to the death of an individual wherein the insured is the applicant and owner and/or the premium payor, that the proceeds will be included in that individual's estate.

Totten Trust—Usually established under banking laws, which allow a person to be named as a beneficiary upon the death of an account owner.

Trust—A fiduciary relationship in which one person (the trustee) is the holder of the legal title to property (the trust property), subject to an equitable obligation to keep or use the property for the benefit of another (the beneficiary).

Trust Company—A corporation, of which one stated objective is to engage in trust business for both individuals and business organizations.

Trustee—An individual or a trust institution that holds the legal title to property for the benefit of someone else, who is the beneficial owner.

Trustor—A person who creates a trust; a broad term that includes *settlor, testator,* or *grantor.*

Undue Influence—The influence that one person exerts over another person to the point where the second person is prevented from exercising his or her own free will.

Uniform Gift to Minors Act (UGMA)—This is always state law and many differ as to how it is to be managed and distributed.

Valuation Date—For Federal estate tax purposes, the value of estate property is held to be its fair market value on the date of the decedent's death or six months after the date of death. The determination is the responsibility of the legal representative.

Vest—To confer an immediate, fixed right of immediate or future possession and enjoyment of property.

Waiver—The voluntary relinquishment of a right, privilege, or advantage. The instrument evidencing the act is also known as *waiver.*

Will—A legally enforceable declaration of a person's wishes regarding matters to be attended to after his or her death and inoperative until his or her death. A will usually, but not always, relates to the testator's property, is revocable or amendable by means of a codicil up to the time of the person's death, and is applicable to the situation that exists at the time of his or her death.

APPENDICES

The following appendices should serve as guidelines to your living trust and related documents. By way of disclaimer, the information contained in these samples is general information and should not be construed as legal advice to be applied to any specific factual situation. The use of the materials in these samples foes not constitute an attorney-client relationship between the user of these materials and the author, or any person or entity related to the author. As the law differs in each legal jurisdiction and may be interpreted or applied differently according to the location or situation, you should not rely on the materials provided in these examples without consulting with an experienced attorney with respect to your specific facts or situation.

APPENDIX A

SAMPLE FIRST PAGE OF REVOCABLE TRUST WITH FULL TABLE OF CONTENTS

NAME OF HUSBAND

AND

NAME OF WIFE

FAMILY TRUST

Reference in this Trust to the "Trustee" shall be deemed a reference to whomever is serving as Trustee, Co-Trustees, whether original, alternate, or successor.

The initial primary Beneficiaries of this Trust Estate shall be (NAME OF HUSBAND) and (NAME OF WIFE).

The effective date of this Trust shall be the date of the signing of this Trust Agreement.

I.   TRUST PROPERTY

    A.   Original Trust Estate

The Trustors acknowledge that they have transferred to the Trustee without consideration the sum of Fifty and no/100 Dollars ($50.00) which was the original corpus of the Trust Estate.

    B.   Additions to Trust Estate

Additional property may be added to the Trust Estate at any time by the Trustors or either of them, or by any person or persons, by inter vivos or testamentary transfer. All such original and additional property is referred to herein collectively as the Trust Estate, and shall be held managed and distributed as herein provided.

TABLE OF CONTENTS

     A. Original Trust Estate
     B. Additions to Trust Estate

        1. Employee Benefit Plans
        2. Life Insurance

           (a) Trustee Named as Beneficiary
           (b) Policy Ownership

     C. Character of Property Unchanged

        1. Community Property Considerations
        2. Retention of Property Character
        3. Gifts Treated as Revocation

II. ORIGINAL AND SUCCESSOR TRUSTEES

     A. Original Co-Trustees
     B. Death or Resignation of Original Co-Trustees
     C. Discharge or Replacement of Trustee by Survivor
     D. Discharge or Replacements of Trustee by Beneficiaries
     E. Approval of Accounts by Beneficiaries
     F. Resignation of a Trustee
     G. Incapacity of a Trustee
     H. Merger of a Corporate Trustee
     I. Limitation of Duties and Responsibilities of Successor Trustees
     J. Authorization and Limitation for Trustee to Modify Language
     K. Bond

III. INITIAL TRUST

     A. Trust Management and Distribution of Income
     B. Distribution of Principal

IV.   REVOCATION AND AMENDMENT

    A. Rights of Revocation
    B. Rights to Amend
    C. Power to Revoke or Amend for Incompetent
    D. Rights of Survivor to Amend or Revoke
    E. Determination of Revocability or Irrevocability

V.   DISTRIBUTIONS ON DEATH OF EITHER TRUSTOR

    A. Decedent's Trust
    B. Survivor's Trust
    C. Other Transfers
    D. Distributions in Cash or Kind

VI.   DECEDENT'S TRUST

    A. Distribution of Income
    B. Distribution of Principal
    C. Survivor's Power of Appointment
    D. Death of Survivor
    E. Trust Irrevocable

VII.   SUVIVOR'S TRUST

    A. Distribution of Income to Survivor
    B. Powers of Appointment of Principal During Life of Survivor
    C. Power of Appointment Upon Death of Survivor
    D. Death of Survivor
    E. Trust Revocable

VIII.   DISTRIBUTION OF TRUST ESTATE

    A. Specific Gift of Real Property to SON AND/OR DAUGHTER'S NAME
    B. Specific Gift of Real Property to SON AND/OR DAUGHTER'S NAME

C. Distribution of Trust Estate

   1. Distribution to DAUGHTER'S NAME
   2. Distribution to DAUGHTER'S NAME
   3. Distribution to SON'S NAME
   4. Distribution to SON'S NAME

D. Discretion Given to Trustee to Avoid Generation-Skipping Tax
E. Termination

   1. No Beneficiaries Surviving
   2. Discretionary Termination
   3. Mandatory Termination
   4. Termination of Trust

F. Trust Irrevocable

IX. SUPPORT AND MAINTENANCE

A. Standard
B. Evidence of Need
C. Preference
D. Guardian's and Conservator's Expenditures

X. DEPOSITORY INTENT OF TRUSTORS AND SPECIFIC
PROVISION FOR DISINHERITANCE AND
CONFIDENTIALITY

A. Disclosure by Trustee
B. Trustors' Intent Regarding Distribution
C. Trustors' Intent Regarding Confidentiality
D. Specific Disinheritance
E. Contest
F. Limitation of Examination of Trust
G. All Settlements Discouraged

XI. TRUST POWERS

A. Introduction

   1. Inclusion of Prudent-Man Rule

B. Management Powers

    1. General Property Powers
    2. Authority to Grant Power of Attorney
    3. Determination of Income and Principal
    4. Loans

       (a) To Trust
       (b) To Beneficiaries

    5. Power to Engage Agents and Professional Services
    6. Right of Trustee to Petition Court
    7. Trustee Authority Regarding Trust Divisions
    8. Right to Receive Annuities and Pension Funds
    9. Transactions Between Trusts
    10. Transactions with Probate Estates of Trustors
    11. Use of Home
    12. Power of Co-Trustees to Act Independently

C. Investment Powers

    1. General
    2. Powers Regarding Real Estate
    3. Authority to Borrow and Repay Loans
    4. Authority to Encumber and Pledge Trust Property
    5. Authority to Sign Debt and Security Documents
    6. Powers Regarding Securities
    7. Powers to Invest in Special Funds
    8. Exercise Stock Options
    9. Authority Regarding Life Insurance and Annuities and Casualty Insurance

D. Administrative Powers

    1. Distributions to or for a Minor or Incompetent
    2. Powers Regarding Taxes and Estate Expenses
    3. Adjustment for Tax Consequences

XIII.   PRESUMPTIONS AND BURDENS OF PROOF

    A. Presumptions
    B. Burden of Proof

APPENDIX B-1

SAMPLE WILLS OF HUSBAND AND CHILDREN
FOLLOWED BY TABLE OF CONTENTS

LAST WILL AND

TESTAMENT

OF

NAME OF HUSBAND

I, NAME OF HUSBAND, residing in the County of _____,
State of _____, being of sound and disposing mind
and memory and not acting under duress, menace, fraud, or undue
influence of any person whomsoever, do hereby make, ordain, publish,
and declare this to be my Last Will and Testament, hereby revoking all
other and former Wills and Codicils to Wills heretofore made by me.

I
MARITAL AND FAMILY STATUS

I declare that I am a married man and that my Wife's name is NAME OF
WIFE; that we have one (1) child of the marriage, namely, NAME OF
CHILD(REN).

II
STATEMENT OF INTENTION

I intend by the terms of this Will to dispose of my entire estate of myself.
I hereby intend to exercise all powers of appointment exercisable by
Will which I now possess or which may hereafter be conferred on me.

TABLE OF CONTENTS

III.   DISPOSTIION OF ENTIRE ESTATE
IV.   OMISSION OF HEIRS
V.   SAVINGS CLAUSE
VI.   APPOINTMENT OF EXECUTOR
VII.   PAYMENT OF DEBTS AND TAXES
VIII.   APPOINTMENT OF TESTAMENTARY GUARDIAN
IX.   EXECUTION OF WILL

APPENDIX B-2

SAMPLE WILLS OF WIFE WITH CHILDREN
FOLLOWED BY TABLE OF CONTENTS

LAST WILL AND

TESTAMENT

OF

NAME OF WIFE

I, NAME OF WIFE, residing in the County of _____, State of _____, being of sound and disposing mind and memory and not acting under duress, menace, fraud, or undue influence of any person whomsoever, do hereby make, ordain, publish, and declare this to be my Last Will and Testament, hereby revoking all other and former Wills and Codicils to Wills heretofore made by me.

I
MARITAL AND FAMILY STATUS

I declare that I am a married woman and that my Husband's name is NAME OF HUSBAND; that we have one (1) child of the marriage, namely, NAME OF CHILD(REN).

II
STATEMENT OF INTENTION

I intend by the terms of this Will to dispose of my entire estate of myself. I hereby intend to exercise all powers of appointment exercisable by Will which I now possess or which may hereafter be conferred on me.

TABLE OF CONTENTS

APPENDIX C

SAMPLE OF BEGINNING SECTION OF DURABLE POWER OF ATTORNEY FOR HEALTH CARE FOLLOWED BY TABLE OF CONTENTS

I
DESIGNATION OF HEALTH CARE AGENT

I, NAME OF HUSBAND/WIFE, a resident of _____County, State of _____, do hereby designate and appoint NAME OF HUSBAND/WIFE as my Agent to make health care decisions for me as authorized in this document. For the purposes of this document, "health care decision" means consent, refusal of consent, or withdrawal of consent to any care, treatment, service, or procedure to maintain, diagnose, or treat an individual's physical or mental condition.

TABLE OF CONTENTS

6. Execute Documents, Enter into Contracts, and Pay Reasonable Compensation or Costs in Implementing the Above Powers

VI. INSPECTION AND DISCLOSURE OF INFORMATION RELATING TO MY PHYSICAL OR MENTAL HEALTH
VII. SIGNING DOCUMENTS, WAIVERS, AND RELEASES
VIII. DETERMINATION OF INCAPACITY AND CAPACITY
IX. DURATION
X. NOMINATION OF CONSERVATOR OF PERSON
XI. ARRANGE MY FUNERAL, BURIAL, OR CREMATION AND MAKE ANATOMICAL GIFTS
XII. AUTOPSY; ANATOMICAL GIFTS; DISPOSTION OF REMAINS
XIII. SPECIAL PERSONAL INSTRUCITONS AND LIMITATIONS
XIV. MISCELLANEOUS PROVISIONS

A. Counterparts
B. Severability
C. Exculpation
D. Governing Law

XV. PRIOR DESIGNATIONS REVOKED

APPENDIX D

SAMPLE LIVING WILL DIRECTIVE,
AKA DIRECTIVE TO PHYSICIANS,
OR DO NOT RESUSCITATE

LIVING WILL DECLARATION
OF
NAME OF HUSBAND/WIFE

TO MY FAMILY, ALL LEGAL AUTHORITY, CLERGY,
PHYSICIANS, AND TO WHOMEVER ELSE MAY READ THIS

DECLARATION

I, NAME OF HUSBAND/WIFE, being of sound mind, willfully and voluntarily make known my desires with an understanding of the full import of this Declaration and declare that I am emotionally and mentally competent to make this Declaration and that it is my desire that my life shall not be artificially prolonged under the circumstances set forth hereafter.

I DO HEREBY DECLARE:

1. If I should have an incurable and irreversible condition that has been diagnosed by two (2) Physicians using reasonable medical judgment; and,
2. If such condition has been diagnosed as resulting in my death within a relatively short time without the administration of life-sustaining treatment, procedures, or devices; or,
3. If I have been found to have an irreversible coma or persistent vegetative state; and,
4. If I am no longer able to make decisions regarding my medical treatment,

I direct that the withdrawal or withholding of medical treatment shall include the use of any procedures, interventions, and devices of any kind or nature, including artificially administered nutrition and hydration that will only prolong the process of dying, or the irreversible coma, or the persistent vegetative state.

NOTWITHSTANDING THE FOREGOING, my Physician is authorized to provide any reasonable assistance to maximize my personal comfort and to alleviate pain in the process of dying.

I further declare that this Declaration shall have a continuing full force and effect whether or not my condition is such that I can no longer directly participate in the decision-making process of life-sustaining procedures. My Physician is to assume that this Declaration is a final expression of my legal right to refuse all medical procedures, interventions, devices of any kind and nature, surgical treatment, nutrition and/or hydration as hereinbefore specified and I do hereby accept the consequences of such stated refusal.

Signed this _____ day of _____, 2012.

_____
NAME OF HUSBAND/WIFE

ACKNOWLEDGMENT

STATE OF _____   )
) ss.
COUNTY OF _____   )

On _____, 2012, before me,_____, a Notary Public, personally appeared NAME OF HUSBAND/WIFE, who proved to me on the basis of satisfactory evidence to be the person whose name is subscribed to the within instrument and acknowledged to me that he executed the same in his authorized capacity, and that by his signature on the instrument the person, or the entity upon behalf of which the person acted, executed the instrument.

I certify under PENALTY OF PERJURY under the laws of the State of _____ that the foregoing paragraph is true and correct.

WITNESS my hand and official seal.

Signature _____ (Seal)

A PHYSICIAN OR OTHER HEALTH CARE PROVIDER WHO IS FURNISHED A COPY OF THE DECLARATION SHALL MAKE IT A PART OF THE DECLARANT'S MEDICAL RECORD AND, IF UNWILLING TO COMPLY WITH THE DECLARATION, PROMPTLY SO ADVISE THE DECLARANT.

APPENDIX E

SAMPLE BURIAL DIRECTIVE
FOLLOWED BY TABLE OF CONTENTS

LETTER OF BURIAL INSTRUCTIONS

FOR

NAME OF HUSBAND/WIFE

I, NAME OF HUSBAND/WIFE, state and declare:

I
FUNERAL SERVICE

I direct that a Service be held in accordance with the desires of my Family.

II
BURIAL DIRECTIONS

I direct that, upon my death, my body be interred at Rose Hills Cemetery.

III
DUPLICATE ORIGINALS

These Instructions are being prepared and executed in duplicate with one (1) set being kept with my original Will and a duplicate original (which is to be given full force and effect) being deposited with my Attorney, _____, of _____, _____.

TABLE OF CONTENTS

APPENDIX F

SAMPLE CREMATION DIRECTIVE
FOLLOWED BY TABLE OF CONTENTS

LETTER OF CREMATION INSTRUCTIONS

FOR

NAME OF HUSBAND/WIFE

I, NAME OF HUSBAND/WIFE, state and declare:

I
FUNERAL SERVICE

I direct that a Service be held in accordance with the desires of my Family.

II
CREMATION

I direct that, upon my death, my body be cremated and my ashes be disposed of in accordance with the desires of my Family.

III
DUPLICATE ORIGINALS

These Instructions are being prepared and executed in duplicate with one (1) set being kept with my original Will and a duplicate original (which is to be given full force and effect) being deposited with my Attorney, _____ of _____,
_____ .

TABLE OF CONTENTS

I.   FUNERAL SERVICE
II.   CREMATION
III.   DUBPLICATE ORIGINALS
IV.   LEGAL AUTHORITY

APPENDIX G

SAMPLE DECLARATION OF PROPERTY OF CHARACTER FOLLOWED BY TABLE OF CONTENTS

THIS DECLARATION, made by and between us, NAME OF HUSBAND and NAME OF WIFE, Husband and Wife, is entered into to specify the ownership of our property as such ownership exists at the date of the execution of this Declaration.

I
Definition of Property Rights

In order to avoid confusion and provide a clear record of our mutual understanding and intent with respect to our past, present, and future transactions regarding the form of property holdings, this shall apply to what has been, is, or may in the future be our sole and separate property or community property.

This Declaration is to record the agreement heretofore understood and now reaffirmed between us, that regardless of the former ownership in which any of our properties have been held, are presently held, or may in the future be held, this Declaration shall dictate our property ownership rights, categorized as either the community property, quasi-community property, or separate property of the named individual.

II
Declaration of Property Character of Husband

We hereby acknowledge that all property listed on Schedule A, attached hereto and incorporated herein by reference, is the sole and separate property of NAME OF HUSBAND having been acquired prior to the time of marriage, or by gift or devise, or by mutual agreement.

III
Declaration of Property Character of Wife

We hereby also acknowledge that all property listed on Schedule B, attached hereto and incorporated herein by reference, is the sole and separate property of NAME OF WIFE, having been acquired prior to the time of marriage, or by gift or devise, or by mutual agreement.

IV
Form of Title Holding Subject to the Agreement
We further acknowledge that since the date of our marriage, for reasons of convenience in managing and handling the properties and without an intent to transfer interest therein between one another, we have in the past and/or may in the future take record title in one or both of our names, or in the name of a Nominee, or in the name of a Trust Agreement which may be either Revocable or Irrevocable, or hold such property in Joint Tenancy form, all such activity being done without any intent of destroying the character of the property as specified herein.

V
Imposed Presumption
Any property not specifically listed on either Schedule A or Schedule B is hereby acknowledged to be our community property.

IN WITNESS WHEREOF, we have hereto signed this Declaration this _____ day of _____, 2012.

_____
NAME OF HUSBAND

_____
NAME OF WIFE

ACKNOWLEDGMENT

STATE OF _____   )
) ss.
COUNTY OF _____   )

On _____, 2012, before me, _____,
a Notary Public, personally appeared NAME OF HUSBAND and NAME
OF WIFE, who proved to me on the basis of satisfactory evidence to be the
persons whose names are subscribed to the within instrument and
acknowledged to me that they executed the same in their authorized
capacities, and that by their signatures on the instrument the persons, or the
entity upon behalf of which the persons acted, executed the instrument.

I certify under PENALTY OF PERJURY under the laws of the State of
_____ that the foregoing paragraph is true and correct.

WITNESS my hand and official seal.

Signature _____ (Seal)

SCHEDULE A

_____

_____

_____

_____

_____

_____

_____

_____

_____

_____

_____

SCHEDULE A

SCHEDULE B

_____

_____

_____

_____

_____

_____

_____

_____

_____

_____

_____

SCHEDULE B

APPENDIX H

SAMPLE LETTER OF INSTRUCTIONS
FOLLOWED BY TABLE OF CONTENTS

Dear Name of Husband/Wife:

This letter is to provide you with information regarding the transfer of assets to your Revocable Living Trust.

NAME OF THE TRUST
The name in which the assets should be held is as follows:

>   Name of Husband and Wife,
>   Co-Trustees, U/D/T Date of Trust,
>   F/B/O Name of Family Trust

This is basically the form which we recommend be used for holding all property under the Trust. As a practical matter, some institutions may require slightly different wording. But the substance should be there; that is, an indication of the Trustee, the date of execution of the Trust, and the beneficiary (ies) or class of beneficiaries.

We believe that the wording has been condensed as much as is possible. The designation "U/D/T" means "under declaration of trust". The designation "F/B/O" means "for the benefit of".

INITIAL ASSETS TO ESTABLISH TRUST

Historically, Trust Law has dictated that for a Trust to come into formal existence it must receive some form of asset. To accomplish this, at the time you signed the initial Trust Agreement and other documents, you also signed an "Assignment of Personal Property" to you as Co-Trustees.

This is sufficient for purposes of establishing the initial corpus of the Trust.

NAMING THE TRUST AS BENEFICIARY

In those situations where life insurance or other assets will name the Trust as the Beneficiary, it is recommended that the following verbiage be used:

> Trustee of Name of Family Trust
> U/D/T date of Trust,
> F/B/O Name of Family

Some insurance companies, and/or other financial institutions have a preprinted form to be completed. The form may be different than the recommended name given above. If the form is particularly unusual and materially different than what we have suggested, we recommend the document be submitted to our office for review before it is finalized.

Also, it is not unusual for some insurance companies to require at the end of the designation we have given, that the phrase "or any other Trustee therein named" be used. This is perfectly acceptable.

FORMAL INSTRUCTIONAL MATERIAL

For your convenience in transferring assets which may be owned by the two of you as Husband and Wife or by either of you as individuals not only at the present time or in the future, we have attached a document entitled, Instructions for Transferring Assets to Trust. You may find that some of the transfers may have already been accomplished. However, we have found from past experience that providing a client with detailed instructional material minimizes confusion on how newly acquired assets should be held as well as making the initial transfer of existing assets to the Trust.

We recognize that the document may not cover every situation. We invite you to contact us if there are any questions either at the present time as to how assets should be transferred to the Trust, or any time in the future as new assets are being acquired.

COST OF MAKING THE TRANSFERS

In making various transfers to your Trust as outlined in the written material or which have been personally discussed with you, our office will charge you according to the time and effort required. The number of transfers in which we became involved will be charged on an hourly basis.

However, the cost of transferring assets to the Trust normally is not a large expenditure.

GENERAL INFORMATION REGARDING SETTLEMENT OF ESTATES

Past experience has shown that the settlement of an Estate is always easier when the assets of the family have been transferred to the Trust in accordance with the directions given.

In situations where the Estate has been fully funded, that is, the assets were transferred to the Trust during life-time, the complexity and cost of settlement of the Estate is minimized.

CAUTION

SIMPLY HAVING A TRUST DOES NOT AVOID PROBATE

The purpose of this letter and the written instructions is to inform you of the ways to transfer assets to your Trust. Also, it is hoped that it will serve to remind you of the consequences which you and your family will face if assets are not transferred to the Trust prior to the time of death.

We hope that you will take full advantage of your Estate Planning. We have done our best to make available to you all the basic Tax advantages and methods to avoid Probate. However, if you have not transferred each and every asset to your Trust, except Joint Tenancy Checking Accounts and motor vehicles, you and your family may be faced with a protracted time of estate settlement and significantly higher costs.

If you have questions, please contact our office.

Respectfully,

Name of Attorney

TABLE OF COTENTS

APPENDIX I

SAMPLE DECLARATION REGARDING ESTATE SPLIT
FOR HUSBAND AND WIFE ON FIRST DEATH
FOLLOWED BY TABLE OF CONTENTS

DECLARATION REGARDING ESTATE SPLIT

THE [**LAST NAME**] FAMILY TRUST

DATED [**DATE OF TRUST**]

I, [**SURVIVING SPOUSE NAME**], state and declare:

1. I am the sole surviving Trustor-Trustee of the [**HUSBAND'S NAME**] and [**WIFE'S NAME**] FAMILY TRUST created by Trust Agreement dated [**DATE OF TRUST**], as amended _____, [**year**], and on _____, [**year**], in its entirety and entered into by and between the undersigned and [**DECEDENT'S NAME**] (Husband and Wife) for the benefit of the [**LAST NAME**] FAMILY.

2. [**DECEDENT'S NAME**], the former Co-Trustor and Co-Trustee of the [**LAST NAME**] FAMILY TRUST AGREEMENT, died on [**DATE OF DEATH**]. **His/Her** Social Security Number was [**SOCIAL SECURITY NUMBER**].

3. Effective as of [**DATE OF DEATH**], and in accordance with the valuations established and reported on Form 706 to the Internal Revenue Service and in accordance with my responsibilities as sole surviving Trustor of the [**LAST NAME**] FAMILY TRUST, I hereby divide the Estate assets into the "DECEDENT'S TRUST" and the "SURVIVOR'S TRUST" in keeping with the terms of the Trust Agreement as found in **ARTICLE V, Distributions on Death of Either Trustor**

4. All assets listed on Exhibit "A", attached hereto, and incorporated herein by reference, are acknowledged to be those assets which are

to be attributed to the DECEDENT'S TRUST as of the date hereof. It is my intention that in accordance with the provisions of ARTICLE V of the Trust Agreement dated **[DATE OF TRUST]**, the assets attributable to the DECEDENT'S TRUST shall equal the total value of one half of the estate- not to exceed the Two Million Dollars ($2,000,000.00) exclusion. This value represents the maximum exclusion under Internal Revenue Code §2010 (c) for the DECEDENT'S TRUST as appraised as of the date of death of **[NAME OF DECEDENT]**.

5. All assets to be attributable to the SURVIVOR'S TRUST, which is revocable, are indicated on Exhibit "B", attached hereto and incorporated herein by reference.

I declare the foregoing statements to be true and correct under penalty of perjury under the laws of the State of **[NAME OF STATE]**.

IN WITNESS WHEREOF, I have set my hand this _____ day of _____, **[YEAR]**, at _____, **[NAME OF STATE]**.

_____

[NAME OF SURVIVOR]
Successor Trustee

ACKNOWLEDGMENT

STATE OF **[NAME OF STATE]**   )
)ss.
COUNTY OF **[NAME OF COUNTY**)

On _____, **[YEAR]**, before me, **[NAME OF NOTARY]**, a Notary Public, personally appeared **[NAME OF SURVIVOR]**, who proved to me on the basis of satisfactory evidence to be the person whose name is subscribed to the within instrument and acknowledged to me that he/she executed the same in his/her authorized capacity, and that by his/her signature on the instrument the person, or the entity upon behalf of which the person acted, executed the instrument.

I certify under PENALTY OF PERJURY under the laws of the State of **[NAME OF STATE]** that the foregoing paragraph is true and correct.

WITNESS my hand and official seal.

Signature _____ (Seal)

EXHIBIT "A"

DECEDENT'S TRUST

INFORMATION ON THIS PAGE IS TO SERVE AS A SAMPLE FOR PREPARING DOCUMENT. PLEASE MAKE SURE TO DELETE INFORMATION WHEN PREPARING FOR CLIENTS.

DESCRIPTION OF PROPERTY	FAIR MARKET VALUE
1. Improved real property located at 2434 Glendower Avenue Los Angeles, CA 90027 APN: 5588-023-008 Less - Debt $445,067.00	$1,754,933.00
2. Furniture, Furnishings, and Collectibles	$210,800.00
3. Cash	$34,267.00
Total	$2,000,000.00

EXHIBIT "B"

SURVIVOR'S TRUST

DESCRIPTION OF PROPERTY   **VALUE**

ALL THE REST OF THE RESIDUE OF
THE ASSETS OF THE ESTATE SHALL
BE ALLOCATED TO THE SURVIVOR'S
TRUST

OR

LIST OF SPECIFIC ASSETS TO BE
INCLUDED IN SURVIVOR'S TRUST

TABLE OF CONTENTS

ABOUT THE AUTHOR

Born in a western mining town in Montana, George M. Turner developed an early recognition of life demanding a passion for work. This was further enhanced by his father, who required him to listen to the New York Symphony, under Conductor Arturo Toscanini, for two hours every Saturday.

Upon the death of Toscanini, the announcer interviewed his son, and asked him "What was the most important thing in your father's life?" To this, he responded with "the most important thing in my father's life was what he was doing at the time he was doing it." This became the hallmark of Mr. Turner's life and his writings.

Mr. Turner's first job out of high school was working in one of the infamous underground mines in Butte, Montana. He then serviced his church as a full-time missionary for two years.

Prior to law school, he worked as an advisor to the field force for New York Life Insurance Company, providing training for sales personnel.

In the mid-eighties, Mr. Turner was hired by a major insurance company in London and became the executive officer of an international insurance company situated in London and Guernsey. It was about the same time he was invited to be a professional writer, and has been writing for more than thirty-one years and has produced over eight volumes of work on various aspects of revocable trusts, irrevocable trusts, and trust administration, and fiduciary responsibility.

Mr. Turner has worked for simplicity and to help the attorney understand that there is a need to explain what can be a very complicated subject, in a form that can be understood by all.

He soon recognized that the fundamentals of estate planning could be reduced to two simple subjects. The first was the issue concerning the individual's person and the second, was the issue concerning the individual's wealth. This is the foundation of the book you are now reading.

The result is a work not buried in the morass of the common law, but an enlightened approach of a public book that is readable and usable for all.

An exclusive benefit to the purchasers of the book:

The author, George M. Turner, would like to be available personally to answer any questions regarding the subject matter therein. Mr. Turner's email address is info@georgemturner.com. Please refer to the book in the subject line. He will respond via e-mail.

Also, please reference these other useful resources for additional information on the topic:

- *Revocable Trusts* – (4 Volumes)
  West Publishing, 5th Edition, 2004
  (West, a Thomson Reuters business)
  Rochester, New York
  (Updated annually)

- *Irrevocable Trusts* – (2 Volumes)
  West Publishing, 3rd Edition, 1996
  (West, a Thomson Reuters business)
  Rochester, New York
  (Updated annually)